TOWARD A RENAISSANCE OF PUERTO RICAN STUDIES:
Ethnic and Area Studies in University Education

María E. Sánchez
Antonio M. Stevens-Arroyo
Editors

Social Science Monographs, Boulder, Colorado
Atlantic Research and Publications, Inc.
Highland Lakes, New Jersey

Distributed by Columbia University Press
1987

ATLANTIC STUDIES ON SOCIETY IN CHANGE

No. 37

Editor-in-Chief Béla K. Király
Associate Editor Peter Pastor
Assistant Editor Albert A. Nofi

Contents

Acknowledgements

The Program on Society in Change conducts research, organizes conferences, and publishes scholarly books. It has been encouraged and supported by Brooklyn College. The National Endowment for the Humanities awarded it a research grant for 1978–81 and renewed it for another three year term (1981–84). Without this substantial and much appreciated support, the Program would not exist. Additional contributions helped us in completing the research, holding conferences, and covering the costs of preparation of the manuscript for publication. Financial aid was granted by the International Research and Exchanges Board, the Open Society Fund and other institutions.

The copy editing was done by Roberto Cambria, and the preparation of the manuscript for publication by Albert A. Nofi, Dorothy Meyerson, Jonathan A. Chanis, and Maurice Leibenstern of the Brooklyn College Program on Society in Change.

To all these institutions and personalities, I wish to express my most sincere appreciation and thanks.

Highland Lakes, New Jersey   Béla K. Király
August 20, 1987   Professor Emeritus of History
Editor-in-Chief

Preface

Born of a national trend toward the recognition of ethnic diversity during the late 60s and early 70s, departments of Puerto Rican Studies have matured into integral academic units of American colleges and universities. During the early years of their existence, these programs pioneered in the creation of a new interdisciplinary field of study and succeeded in representing the interests of a community of students, faculty, and alumni. In the process, these departments also struggled for autonomy, internal consolidation, and the elaboration of a philosophy and direction that grew out of this praxis.

The initial period was characterized by a zeal and activism that still permeates the more developed and established programs. However, as the 80s approached and a different ideological climate began to reshape the academic agenda of the universities, Puerto Rican Studies began to lose "relevance" as the ethnic revival of the 60s was coming to a close. This then spurred academics and community activists alike toward a consciousness of this new reality. To this effect, and on its tenth anniversary, the Department of Puerto Rican Studies at Brooklyn College initiated a process of introspection and analysis aimed at the assessment of our collective efforts during the formative years of the discipline.

The conference format was agreed upon as an appropriate vehicle for the culmination of this assessment, while also providing a broad forum to chart the future orientation of Puerto Rican Studies as a field.

The materials included in this volume synthesize the academic experience of Puerto Rican Studies programs in the American university setting. The core of the selected essays are adaptations of papers delivered at a conference held at Brooklyn College on April 3-4, 1981, entitled "Renaissance of Puerto Rican Studies: An Agenda for the Eighties."

The introduction documents the origins of Puerto Rican Studies, the present status of the field, and future projections and challenges.

The eleven essays which follow conceptualize and discuss the functions of Puerto Rican Studies and present a vision of the curriculum within an inter- and multi-disciplinary approach. The concluding essays concentrate on reflections and an action agenda for these programs in the eighties. Finally, the volume closes with an epilogue that suggests a renaissance and redefinition of Puerto Rican Studies.

It is hoped that these presentations will serve as tools for discussion and analysis, and promote a broader understanding of the legitimacy and place of Puerto Rican Studies as an academic field.

We wish to acknowledge the hard work and dedication of the faculty and staff of the Puerto Rican Studies Department at Brooklyn College, namely: Professor Antonio Stevens-Arroyo, conference coordinator; Professors Hector Carrasquillo and Virginia Sanchez-Korrol, and Mildred Nieves-Rivera, departmental secretary.

Special thanks are extended to President Robert L. Hess for his support and efforts at securing financial resources.

Our deepest gratitude goes to the Puerto Rican Studies Alumni Association for valuable assistance in the conference and a substantial financial contribution that has made this publication possible. We particularly wish to thank Herminia Ramos-Donovan, Angel Deliz, and Joaquin Rosa. Our final thank-you must be given to the contributors of this volume, for they were commissioned to prepare seminal papers that would be subjected to considerable scrutiny and criticism. Those selected for the task were indeed able to combine gifts of both scholarship and humility in rising to meet this challenge.

April, 1986   Maria E. Sanchez, Chairperson
Department of Puerto Rican Studies   Antonio Nadal, Deputy
Brooklyn College   Chairman
City University of New York

INTRODUCTION

Puerto Rican Studies: Roots and Challenges

Josephine Nieves *et al.*

In 1969, in the wake of campus upheaval, a New York City Board of Higher Education resolution conceded, ". . . it shall be the policy of the City University and its constituent colleges to encourage the development of Black and Puerto Rican Studies within the university, and to give the funding of these programs special priority."[1]

Puerto Ricans had demanded access to higher education and the establishment of ethnic studies programs. We sought a transformation in the nature of higher education itself. Not only had the university virtually excluded Puerto Rican students and faculty, it had also played a major role in distorting our history, and in so doing had misrepresented the history of the United States as well.

The creation of Puerto Rican Studies was part of the social, political, and intellectual development of the Puerto Rican community. Its emergence as a new academic area in higher education was not an isolated achievement. Rather, it was connected to the hard won gains of poor and minority communities across the United States, as well as the insurrections of third world peoples, including the movement for Puerto Rican independence.

For *Boricuas* (Puerto Ricans) in particular, the reality of the movement of Puerto Ricans between the Island and the United States was an important point of reference for our intellectual inquiry in the university. By 1970, the flow of unemployed or underemployed Puerto Ricans set in motion by the varying demands of American capital had not registered any significant gains for our people. For the nearly two million Puerto Ricans concentrated in the declining cities of the Northeast, the persistant problems of high rates of unemployment, deteriorated housing, poor health, and low levels of education provided grim evidence of the similarity of conditions in the continental United

States and in Puerto Rico. As children of successive waves of workers displaced by the profit and production requirements of industrialization, our presence here could only be understood in the context of the Island's colonial relationship to the United States.[2]

Puerto Rican Studies is the most recent example in a long line of organized attempts by Puerto Ricans to resist absorption, to survive as a linguistic and cultural community in the United States, and to advance a collective political and social agenda. If we examine the historical development of Puerto Ricans in the United States, we find emerging a diversity of strategies and ideological views. Particular modes of struggle predominated at given historical periods, reflecting different conditions, understandings, and organizational experiences.

For example, faced with institutional racism and the continuous decline of levels of schooling among Puerto Rican youth, organizations like Aspira and the National Puerto Rican Forum developed in the 1950s with the support of foundations and corporate and government funds. These organizations were created on the premise that the movement out of poverty for an entire community was possible through higher education and leadership development based upon strengthened cultural identity. This assessment continued into the 1960s with the self-help approach of the antipoverty programs. The strategy was one of using formal education as the lever for social mobility; it was based on the belief that social equality and opportunity were possible for all. More often than not, this led to an uncritical striving toward an illusory pattern of success and material reward. While opening up institutions of higher education to some Puerto Ricans and providing a forum for cultural affirmation and cohesion, this approach neither took the majority of our people out of poverty nor brought us into the mainstream.

During the mid-1960s, escalation of the Vietnam War and the draft led to a nationwide student movement against the United States government and institutions of higher education which were linked to the American war effort.[3] Puerto Ricans and other minorities bearing a share of the war effort out of proportion to their numbers also rebelled and sought fundamental change. Organizations such as the Young Lords Party, FUPI (*Federación Universitaria Pro-Independencia*), and the Puerto Rican Student Union are examples of groups that emerged within the United States and on the Island, who espoused open and, if necessary, violent confrontation as a means of challenging the legitimacy of existing institutions and their role in perpetuating inequality. The entire concept of reform as a means of improving our conditions was brought into serious question during this period. Many groups militantly asserted that the community had a right to self-defense against the violence perpetuated on our daily lives—in the workplace, by the government, and by the institutional network of social services.[4] As new organizations and strategies developed in the Puerto Rican community, open conflict commenced at the neighborhood level, in schools and community control struggles, in welfare rights movements, in hospitals, churches, and with law enforcement agencies.

Within this climate of militancy, our approach in higher education meant demanding not only access or entry to the university, but also rejecting an institution which acted against our own interests. Our critique of the university in 1973 centered upon its role in:

1. reproducing class divisions;
2. transmitting the values, traditions, and world views of the dominant class;
3. selecting and preparing an elite to work within a system which legitimates colonization and exploitation;
4. promoting relationships based on hierarchy, authoritarianism, power, and fixed roles;
5. controlling and defining knowledge, and developing research in the interests of a ruling elite.

Puerto Rican Studies was an organizational form through which we challenged the university and created a separate space in which to test and develop our own educational agenda. The commitment of Puerto Rican faculty and students to examine facts or principles in order to act on our condition as a people formed the essence of our intellectual work in the university. Like Black Studies and Chicano Studies, Puerto Rican Studies began with a purpose and content which went beyond intellectualism. The era of social upheaval, community conflict, and demands for institutional change, gave these ethnic programs a stamp and character of social practice and theory building different from most other university programs. Our efforts involved, in particular, a critique of the way social science theory and methods had served to legitimatize our colonial history.[5] Hence, a basic set of principles was almost uniformly established in all colleges:

Autonomy —the demand for separate departments or programs wherein Puerto Ricans would have decision-making power over content of curriculum, hiring of faculty, and direction of policy.

Methodology —a rejection of traditional approaches to learning, a defining of new sources of knowledge stemming from within our own Puerto Rican experience, and an experimentation with collective methods of doing intellectual work.

Theoretical Framework —a discarding of apologist and colonizing ideologies, and the design of theoretical constructs within which to produce fresh analyses about the Puerto Rican condition.

Community Base —an insistence on applying new knowledge and the intellectual capacities and other university resources to struggles and issues in the community, not as intellectual elites but as university-based, intellectual workers.

Puerto Rican Studies courses and programs were introduced in other colleges and universities, but the focal point was the City University of New York (CUNY), which houses the majority of all continental Puerto Rican college students, most of whom are poor and working class. CUNY programs grew from five in the senior colleges in 1969 to seventeen in 1973; from 35 courses in 1969 to 155 in 1973; from 1967 students enrolled in 1969 to 6241 in 1973. By 1973, Puerto Rican instructional staff in CUNY totaled 541.

As we were breaking ground in defining our role in the university, we were also making an impact on the university as a whole. The Open Admissions struggle and ethnic studies programs forced the universities to modify their policy of years of racial exclusion. Universities found themselves in a contradiction: at the same time that they conceded greater access, they encountered a student population that would not relinquish its claims to develop its own class and cultural interests in return for a place in the university. This contradication continues. The university's reluctance to incorporate intellectual work rooted in the class and national interests of a largely working-class community places it in continuing conflict with Puerto Ricans. But in spite of escalating assaults on Puerto Rican Studies, we have maintained our space; departments of Puerto Rican Studies continue to be actual or potential progressive bases from which to build an ongoing and meaningful presence within the university.

The actual impact of Puerto Rican Studies on tens of thousands of Puerto Ricans cannot be easily measured. These programs and the presence of Puerto Ricans in institutions of higher learning have affected the nature and scope of post-secondary education, as well as the lives of the students themselves.

To a certain degree, we have also developed an educational agenda in which activism and scholarship are seen as essential complimentary elements, not opposing forces. This agenda is reflected in materials produced which depart from apologetic theories about the nature of our community. These new analyses have not only deepened our understanding, but have also broken ground in academia in the areas of language, culture, and migration.[6] Thus, for many, Puerto Rican Studies has been an encouraging movement offering the environment for rigorous intellectual work linked to principled political activism. This is an accomplishment, for it serves as a model for all Puerto Ricans engaged in intellectual work and defines more clearly our role in the university.

Puerto Rican Studies has also reached a new level of consciousness about the community's need for skilled and informed individuals. Through its curriculum, faculty and student activities, Puerto Rican Studies has contributed to the formation of a core of Puerto Ricans whose political commitment to collective work and social change is a guiding principle for their work.

Despite these and other impressive achievements, internal and external problems and contradictions have continually threatened the existence of Puerto Rican Studies, and more importantly, its commitment to its original goals. For example, in part because of the scarcity of experienced Puerto Rican academics in the United States, students turned uncritically to Puerto Rico for recruitment of faculty. Unanticipated conflicts and tensions arose out of the differences in class background, cultural experiences, aspirations, and political outlooks of Island faculty and U.S.-born students.

Other problem areas have included the tensions between traditional academic practices and new approaches in teaching, collective decision-making, and work in the community as defined by the working-class experience and political objectives of the students. These tensions have at times thwarted careful examination and full development of theoretical understanding about Puerto Rican conditions and about methodologies for producing knowledge and learning.

By 1975, barely six years after the Board of Higher Education's first statement supporting Black and Puerto Rican Studies in CUNY, Chancellor Kibbee declared these programs "prime candidates for elimination." By 1976, decline was apparent: programs were reduced from 17 to 11; full-time faculty in 7 of the programs decreased from 56 to 35 in only two years. With the exception of a few campuses, the erosion of the university's commitment to these programs was clear.

As students and faculty struggled to survive the university attacks and day-to-day crises, our lack of experience and ideological fervor also led to unreasonable expectations and excessive demands on ourselves. The refinement of a cohesive philosophy and set of principles to guide the formation and direction of new departments became increasingly difficult as each one developed almost independently, with little opportunity, amidst myriad particular sets of problems and meager resources, to coordinate planning and other strategies.

Among the talented, skilled, and committed students and faculty, there were many who risked individual career goals to challenge the university. The retaliation of university officials against these activists brought sanctions that barred their access to, and withheld the credentials necessary for, professional achievement. We understand, however, that those individuals made it possible for many of us to continue our endeavors. They helped build our base in the university and are part of our present development.

Moreover, as state and university retrenchment policies forced drastic cutbacks in operations and personnel, and the political climate began to change in the mid-1970s, the university doubled its efforts to bring Puerto Rican Studies into line. The struggle for survival became constant, inevitably resulting in the departments' internalization of more traditional academic standards. In sum, the institutionalization of Puerto Rican Studies has been both a victory and a defeat. A victory because we affirmed our right to space within the university, where our intellectual work can focus on the needs and concerns of our community. A defeat, because the very struggle for survival, while making us strong, also dissipated energies on goals that were short-term and disconnected to our primary purpose. The search for permanency and legitimacy reflected in the fight for faculty lines, tenure, and academic jurisdiction, tended to become ends in themselves rather than mechanisms to accomplish our objectives of autonomy, an alternate methodology, and ties to the community. The competition imposed by survival has kept the programs fragmented, discouraging alliances with other departments and constituencies, isolating them from one another and from other progressive departments in the colleges. As our programs have become tied defensively to university committees, bureaucratic structures, and elitist criteria, our connection to the community has weakened. Norms and goals reshaped to fit university requirements have made our accountability more and more to the university rather than to the community.

The question of legitimacy for Puerto Rican Studies has become paramount as we have been forced to meet university standards and definitions. Legitimacy in institutional terms essentially means conformity and accommodation to the values and purposes of higher education. Whereas before we had found the values and methods of the university illegitimate, we now seek legitimacy on the university's own terms. Are we more legitimate now because we have acquired more PhD's, or because we have sought tenure, or because we have been distanced from our communities? The central question is: legitimate for whom, for whose benefit, and toward what end?

This process of institutionalization has steadily gained ground. Alliances and compromises are being forced rather than self-defined under threat of absorption through merger with other departments, or virtual elimination through loss of faculty positions, reductions in courses and budgets, the distribution of Puerto Rican Studies courses within traditonal departments, etc. As university efforts mount to reestablish the authority and legitimacy of traditional research and scholarship, the possibilities for growth of Puerto Rican Studies in any direction other than that prescribed by college bureaucrats are being severely limited.

Perhaps more deceptive has been the official recognition and promotion on several campuses of selected aspects of Puerto Rican culture. By providing funds and support for particular projects, a renewed attempt is underway to define as "acceptable" only certain literary and artistic aspects of Puerto Rican culture, in effect isolating them from the political and economic conditions in which they develop.

Part of this policy includes the submergence of ethnic studies programs in larger administrative units fed by smaller budgets. On some campuses, all non-traditonal programs—women's studies, labor studies, Puerto Rican, Black, white ethnic, and even traditional area studies—are merged and forced to compete for greatly reduced funding. This easily creates or reinforces schisms between the various white and minority working-class communities which support these ethnic studies programs. On other campuses, the critical force of Puerto Rican and other oppressed minority studies is diluted by submerging them in larger entities which celebrate the very structure which we criticize.

Both the insertion of Puerto Rican Studies within larger, often hostile departments, and the encouragement of restricted portions of Puerto Rican culture, are justified by a perverse ideological reformulation of "cultural pluralism." This form of cultural pluralism promotes only those modes of ethnic cultural activity which do not question—which leave intact—those components of the U.S. white Anglo-Saxon Protestant class structure and culture which continue to oppress us.

This new "cultural pluralist" philosophy is now being used to submerge and deflect the most critical and fundamental concerns of our community: its economic, cultural, and political survival. Although on the surface this liberal philosophy seems to represent a most viable, intelligent alternative to the forced assimilation expressed in the melting pot model, it is deceptive and must be openly challenged. Cultural pluralism overlooks certain critical socio-economic distinctions between groups that transcend mere cultural differences. If, on the one hand, it purports to give all ethnic groups an equal opportunity to examine and preserve their cultural heritage and cultural folkways, it ignores historical issues and conditions which make for the continued oppression of particular ethnic and racial minorities.

The demands for ethnic studies programs as expressed by the Puerto Rican, Black, Chicano, and Native American communities did not simply call for a "cultural" presence in the university. Puerto Ricans had already recognized the limited social and political effectiveness of rallying around culture or individual economic and social mobility as the key for individuals to pass into a rather dubious marginal middle-class membership. Nor were we seeking to examine our cultural roots in academic solitude and isolation, or to express the romantic need for ethnic revelation. Rather, we have sought admission to the university to examine the critical connections linking our political, economic, social, and cultural realities within the broader socio-economic context of American society.

Puerto Rican Studies and other minority programs have attempted to examine culture within different historical and contemporary realities. Courses in Puerto Rican Studies address issues of colonialism, economic exploitation, creative arts, community rebuilding, institutional racism, housing, educational genocide, health issues, the family, etc. These issues are not part of the cultural pluralist's agenda, because they explode and expose a myth of a cultural diversity confined to apolitical ethnic expression. In contrast, white ethnic studies curricula do not generally seem to focus on economic, class, or racial issues which are a vital part of our core courses. Our concern with ethnicity represents a profoundly different emphasis and thrust. Because of a historical pattern of victimization, we have little faith in a "cultural pluralism" that promotes a facade of ethnic egalitarianism.

Cultural pluralism, as practiced in the university today, has had the effect of significantly muting the urgency of the expressed needs and demands of the Puerto Rican community. It has taken the question of ethnicity out of the political and economic domain and reduced it to a debate about quality of curriculum, tenure, academic solvency, and "cultural" studies.

We have no reason to be grateful to the university for including us in its grand smorgasbord of ethnic culture—we deserve to be in the university in our right. Nor can we trust the efforts of university bureaucrats to merge various ethnic studies without unifying them, or to pit them against one another without drawing the most important distinctions. The unity of oppressed ethnic groups is not a legitimate imposition from above. It is a matter for our own self-definition.

Clearly, as we enter the 1980s, the conditions Puerto Ricans face in the university only mirror the broad attacks on the poor and working class by national and multinational forces for the purposes of economic and political gain. The attacks are severe, cutting across every sphere of our lives—eroding past social progress, destroying basic human rights, closing off even limited avenues for access and advancement.

Yet, the contradictions in the present situation form a base of strength from which to move forward. At the point of severest attack, the level of awareness, expectations, and political experience of our community is also at its height.

These contradictions are clearly evident in the university as well, where, for example, in sheer numbers blacks and Hispanics in CUNY may soon predominate. While tuition increases and regressive screening policies at every level of education may once again exclude large numbers of Puerto Rican youth, the absence of jobs and the need to prevent rebellion may in fact increase our enrollment in colleges and universities. In addition, cutbacks in federal support to higher education, while threatening our possibilities, has called forth widespread resistence from diverse groups—from middle-class parents facing rising tuition to university administrators facing enrollment crises. These forces may push for policies facilitating our participation in higher education. As stratification of post-secondary institutions becomes more severe, and our students are tracked into dead-end careers or revolving door college programs, the seeds of discontent can grow into political consciousness and organized opposition.

The demystification of the university and our increasing knowledge of its function, its structure, its factions and forces, places us at a greater advantage than before in attempting to bring about necessary change. This includes forming alliances with supportive elements as well as with other similarly depressed constituencies—blacks, other Hispanics, Native, and North Americans. The inadequacy of a conservative and liberal philosophy is more and more apparent as the contradictions grow sharper and the generalized effects of attacks on all sectors of the working class will make possible a coalescing of mutual interests. From this growing base of understanding the major forces at work, the task of moving forward in the 1980s remains our collective challenge.

Notes

1. Board of Higher Education of the City of New York. 1969. Minutes of Proceedings. July 5th, S-108.

2. For a full treatment of the relationship between agrarian and industrial capitalism on the Island and the expulsion of labor at various periods of economic development, see Frank Bonilla and Ricardo Campos. "A Wealth of Poor: Puerto Ricans in the New Economic Order." *Daedalus*, 110, Spring, 1981, pp. 133–76; History Task Force, Centro de Estudios Puertorriqueños, *Labor Migration Under Capitalism: The Puerto Rican Experience*, New York: Monthly Review Press, 1979.

3. Details on the relationship between higher education and the war effort can be found in *The University - Military - Police Complex: A Director and Related Documents*, compiled by Michael Klare and published by The North American Congress on Latin America, 1970.

4. Puerto Ricans, as with other minority poor, are subjected to dangerous working conditions, deteriorated housing, forced relocations, poor health conditions, shunning, and downgrading of language differences, inadequate schooling, etc., etc., etc.

5. One example of this critique can be found in History Task Force, Centro de Estudios Puertorriqueños, *Labor Migration Under Capitalism: The Puerto Rican Experience*. New York: Monthly Review Press, 1979, Chapter 1.

6. A more recent example of new analysis in language and culture can be found in Juan Flores, John Attinasi, and Pedro Pedraza, Jr. "La Carreta Made a U-Turn: Puerto Rican Language and Culture in the United States." *Daedalus*, 110, Spring 1981, pp. 193–217.

PART ONE

THE FUNCTIONS OF PUERTO RICAN STUDIES

1

Puerto Rican Studies and the Interdisciplinary Approach

Frank Bonilla

The following remarks are intended to provide a starting point for a discussion that we can only hope to begin. I have attempted to compress and place in context a sizable number of questions suggested by the theme assigned to me. Each point contains assertions, impressions, and tentative conclusions that I expect to illustrate and explain further.

1. Numerous branches of learning or fields of study are actively involved in Puerto Rican Studies. Undeniably, then we are involved in some sense in an interdisciplinary or multidisciplinary enterprise. But what are disciplines and how can they be reconnected once they have established separate identities? One impression hard to avoid is that disciplines are defined simply by their object of study. Biology is the science of living organisms; geology studies the earth and its rocks; physics has to do with matter and motion. But physics, it seems, once encompassed the study of all of nature. It only gradually narrowed to cover chiefly those aspects of the material world that could be studied by certain methods, a combination of the experimental and the quantitative. Today, with notable advances in both the tools for experimentation and mathematics, physics is reabsorbing large portions of sciences, such as those already named, that for decades pursued quite independent paths.[1] Biology and chemistry are in the forefront of incursions into terrain until quite recently thought to be the exclusive province of psychiatry and social science. Thus the boundaries between disciplines and even the larger aggregates into which the academy packages teaching and research (humanities, social sciences, natural sciences) are continually being rearranged through the play of complex social forces that include much more than the objects of science, its methods, or most pressing puzzles. We all know,

for example, that powerful corporate and state interests now mediate all significant realignments of this kind within the so-called "big" or "hard" sciences.

2. It may be easier to see similar forces at work in the emergence or regrouping of disciplines focused on topics closer to our own. American Studies, for example, surfaced as an "interdiscipline" in United States universities in the 1930s. It arose as a movement against the neglect of United States as against British literature and history in WASP-dominated departments of History and English. The move after World War II to integrate and provide a quantitative foundation for the social sciences, which was reflected in the 1950s and 1960s at major universities around the country, was part and parcel of a new vision of the United States' role in global affairs that was to be advanced in part by the mobilization of the best knowledge that human sciences modelled on the natural sciences could produce. This and subsequent interdisciplinary projects had their intellectual manifestos emphasizing the scholarly gains to be had in breadth, sharpness, and sophistication of anticipated research results by pooling the data, concepts and methods of several fields.[2] These hopes have not always been realized. Mathematical sociology, socio-linguistics, socio-biology—all stand today as instances of attempts at fusions of disciplines that continue to be seen as abortive by practitioners on both sides of the fields concerned. Moreover, in moments of more open crisis, as with the opening 1965 number of the *Urban Affairs Quarterly*, the scholarly apparatus has taken second place to the commands of political urgency. This call for an interdisciplinary urban studies is announced with a simple White House directive from Lyndon Johnson: it is time for academics to get on the job and produce some policy perspectives on what is happening in the cities. As we all know, a very different configuration of political forces rallied around the immediately succeeding struggles for Black, Chicano, Puerto Rican, and Women's Studies, and each of these raised quite different challenges to the academy and its established fields.

3. All this by way of preamble to suggest that we need to think through very carefully the matter of academic disciplines and the way in which they may be combined in United States institutions to advance the study of Puerto Rican reality. Do we face just a problem of exclusion or neglect that the university and specific disciplines can readily remedy by turning attention to overlooked subject matters, opening the way to training and research opportunities for a few Puerto Ricans, or taking more seriously the needs of a new clientele? What do we know about why the existing system of knowledge production in the country has served us so poorly? These are truly

complex questions, but we can start from at least one simple premise. Puerto Rican Studies now exist in the United States because consciously or intuitively enough of us *reject any version of education or learning that does not forthrightly affirm that our freedom as a people is a vital concern and an attainable goal.* That is, we have set out to contest effectively those visions of the world that assume or take for granted the inevitability and indefinite duration of the class and colonial oppression that has marked Puerto Rico's history. All the disciplines that we are most directly drawing upon—history, economics, sociology, anthropology, literature, psychology, pedagogy—as they are practiced in the United States are deeply implicated in the construction of that vision of Puerto Ricans as an inferior, submissive people, trapped on the underside of relations from which there is no foreseeable exit.

4. Are United States universities today a place where the project of overturning this vision can be sensibly and usefully advanced? Is anything going on there that has to do with our social advance and eventual liberation? Are we smuggling into the academy work and values that should more appropriately be pursued elsewhere? We can say "yes" to the last question only if we believe that the prospect of our freedom and our intellectual agenda can be moved forward without directly confronting the class and national forces presently in command of the institutions of higher learning where we are beginning to establish a presence. We have to answer "yes" if we are in fact only interlopers and opportunists, unprepared to struggle against the contradictions within the academy and organized disciplines that genuinely hold back the advance of learning and reinforce its oppressive features.

5. Many of these features of United States higher education are being widely denounced and were acknowledged well before we came on the scene. What we need to clarify is the particulars of how these conditions bear on our own learning and research as well as the ways in which we may effectively become part of a genuine counterforce. Do we have anything to offer in lieu of the consuming concern with proprietary interests over knowledge and careerism in the university? How do we respond to the continuing pressures for quick empirical sweeps of "the facts" on fragmented aspects of our situation as models of productive research? What stake, if any, have we in ongoing theoretical disputes in the disciplines that most directly concern us? Should we be echoing the call from on high for pragmatic eclecticism and tolerance among competing weak paradigms in the social sciences? How do we deal with the main obstacles to secure self-knowledge now present in all the disciplines represented here—empiricism, formalism, relativism?

6. I have posed these concerns as questions although I believe that both in the principles we projected at the start of Puerto Rican Studies a decade ago and in our subsequent practice we have essayed tentative answers. My perceptions on the points that follow are necessarily heavily influenced by experience at the Centro, but I am sure you will all have related points to bring out based on the practice in those places where you have lived this process.

a. *Setting the record straight.* An immediate objective in the early period of Puerto Rican Studies was to clear the ground of allegedly scholarly and authoritative versions of Puerto Rican reality that could be shown to be shakily grounded in fact, shallowly supported by theory, and substantially ideological in intent. There has been considerable accomplishment on this front although the job is far from complete. New work, increasingly from within our own ranks, continues to require close critical scrutiny. Some earlier weaknesses of critical efforts—a reactive anti-intellectualism, a dogmatic and over-simplified application of critical concepts, and a certain amount of self-idealization—have been partially overcome. The objective grounds for a more systematic, fine-grained, and genuinely constructive criticism now exist and need to be applied.

b. *Constructing an alternative approach.* We have gained in confidence that a scientific approach to our intellectual goals can be framed— an approach that can grasp the totality of our problematic placement in the present world order, that is sensitive to the rich interconnectedness and contradictory nature of those problems, and that builds from and leads back to our practical movement in the real world. In my view, Marxist theory and concepts are an indispensable keystone in this effort and constitute the essential link in the necessary *transcendence* rather than the mere mechanical reassortment of disciplinary lines. Of course, this still leaves numerous large questions unanswered, since there are many opinions about how this project can be best advanced.

c. *Collectivism and accountability.* Over these years we have gained a certain amount of experience in collective work, in breaking down the individualistic, competitive, and hierarchical habits and structures of the institutions within which we function. At the Centro this practice has been most successful in group decision-making, especially with regard to basic principles and broad priorities. It has also been partially realized in group study, research, in writing for publication, and in matters of group evaluation and individual accountability. It has been least successful in maintaining stable ties to community constituencies and timely involvement from that source at critical junctures. Our ability to project this experience outward to other quarters of the university has been minimal.

d. *Training and self-reproduction.* If the situation in the disciplines now represented in Puerto Rican Studies is approximately as sketched above, we cannot leave the teaching of Puerto Ricans at any level, and especially graduate instruction, entirely to traditional departments, even the more progressive among them. This applies with special force to broad questions of theory, method, and research practice. There can be no lasting change from within this movement in the way Puerto Ricans experience higher education and go on to perform intellectual work unless there is some stable matrix in which new relations in the production and sharing of knowledge can be prefigured and tested.

e. In this connection, the primacy of undergraduate instruction and the integrity and continuity of departments and programs must be kept well in the foreground of our preoccupations. Protecting those programs, keeping research responsive to teaching needs, struggling to provide support, recognition, and opportunities for further development to faculty and students— all are first order priorities in defending and consolidating the modest gains won at such high cost.

f. *Extinction vs. cooptation.* After ten years of struggle for survival, Puerto Rican Studies still faces the hostility and skepticism of traditionalists within the university and the threats of budget trimmers eager for pretexts to wipe out any program not manifestly linked to immediate utilitarian and vocational objectives. Despite a certain vogue of academic Marxism, the application of materialist perspectives to politically sensitive subject matters also continues to irritate and alarm many quarters of the educational establishment. Nevertheless, to the old dangers we must now add the perils of legitimation and cooptation, as the more successful programs and a few practitioners consolidate their positions at institutions here and there. The need for sustained communication, exchange, support, and pulling of coat tails within networks that effectively reach most of us, is now more pressing than ever.

g. *A Puerto Rican contribution to social science.* The contribution that a people may make to the stock of useful kowledge of the world eventuates from a complex admixture of necessity, opportunity, and choice. Wilfredo Mattos in his *La política y lo político en Puerto Rico* asks why Puerto Rico is now a focus of counterrevolution. I would say that is so because we embody some of the gravest contradictions of the present economic and political order, both on an international scale and within the United States. We have objective grounds and powerful motivations to raise issues about that order that other peoples are less well situated to perceive. The task before us is, therefore, to produce a broadly gauged, thorough-going, objectively grounded dialectical understanding of the unique historical situation of Puerto Ricans in today's world. Some central themes in this inquiry have already emerged—the changing nature of colonial relations with the advance of capital on a world scale; the shifting of currents of movement of capital, labor power, and other commodities within and across national boundaries; the interplay of language and culture as filtered through class relations in the process of acculturation and resistance to assimilation. I believe we will advance more directly toward the building of a significant record of intellectual achievement through fruitful attacks on questions of this order than through any programmatic attempt to domesticate or transmute into something comfortably Puerto Rican the conceptual schemes and methods of mainstream United States social disciplines and institutions.

Notes

1. *The Sciences*, March 1981:11.
2. For a good example, see the 1970, first issue of *The Journal of Interdisciplinary History*.

2

Puerto Rican Studies in Higher Education: Growing and Learning Within Conflict and Contradiction

Eduardo Aponte

As academics, we have been assigned the difficult task of cultivating our people's cultural development and of expressing scientifically the consciousness of society. All too often these tasks have led to bitter separation from the daily experience of our Puerto Rican people. Today we hope for a new beginning, a renaissance.

Puerto Rican Studies is institutional divisions of the university which were born out of conflict over our society's unequal social relations. Consequently, Puerto Rican Studies will reproduce conflict and contradications in the United States until a multicultural partic004 ipatory democracy is achieved. Moreover, forces alien to the best interests of the Puerto Rican people intend to eliminate or coopt our departments and programs as has unfortunately occurred with similar ethnic and minority programs. Nonetheless, Puerto Rican Studies remains an important educational agent devoted to the critical study, cultural transmission, and development of the Puerto Ricans in the United States and Puerto Rico.

There are several functions that Puerto Rican Studies performs; all of them operative within the unequal social relationships and contradictions of society and its institutions. Our focus in the presentation will be on three main functions. First, the enculturation or cultural transmission which is the process necessary to transmit, critically interpret, and develop the Puerto Rican cultural tradition. Secondly, the task of insuring that graduates of Puerto Rican Studies are equipped with the attributes and attitudes relevant to the pursuit of a professional career. (Let us assume that professional knowledge and skills are provided by the general university education.) Thirdly, Puerto Rican Studies should continue previous political socialization—

by this I mean the acquisition of political consciousness and an ideology.

These three tasks must respond to the situational needs and struggle of our people for equality and the establishment of a multicultural society.

Puerto Rican Studies has always functioned within contradictions. One, by introducing Puerto Rican Studies to the university, our people's struggle for equality has been institutionalized within higher education. Thus, together with ethnic studies, our departments and programs represent an enculturation process within society's majority. Inevitably, what appears as an assertion of pluralism also acquires a second and contradictory function of acculturation, assimilating distinct values and goals to the demands of the total society. For example, a Puerto Rican Studies major at Brooklyn College requires approximately one-third of the total university credits to be taken within the Puerto Rican Studies Department. But while students dedicate 33 percent of their study and class time to Puerto Rican Studies, they continue to be subject to the acculturating forces of United States society at home, in the community, and at work, as well as in the university itself. This means that the time and scope of enculturation—the counter-acculturation process—is proportionately less than the forces working toward assimilation in some form. Two, there is a conflict between the conformist political socialization of the broader university curriculum and the lesser but intensive consciousness-raising of the Puerto Rican Studies curriculum. Our curriculum provides a perspective on the political and economic contradictions affecting our people and on the modes of action against oppression. Three, the demands of the broader university curriculum that reflect society's unequal social relationships conflict with the Puerto Rican community's needs for skilled professionals who are also community oriented, and sensitive to Puerto Rican problems and socio-economic needs. Finally, we must recognize that we might lose the struggle for an effective Puerto Rican Studies, but not on that account capitulate to co-optation. This is the fourth conflict about the function of Puerto Rican Studies and one that is likely to be internalized by those of us most directly involved with administration and teaching. For example, do we explain declining enrollments by referring to the general decline in the eligible college population in the United States? Or rather do we accept as partly our own responsibility the fact that fewer students look to higher education as a part of their career preparation? Our renaissance begins when we assume this responsibility not only for our departments but also for the entire university. Only in this way, it would seem to me, can we master the fourth conflict and avoid becoming a token program destined to disappear.

A renaissance of Puerto Rican Studies will entail the re-establishment of conflict at the university. Such a conflict need not be physical and destructive: rather it must be centered on the struggle to create a curriculum in the university relevant to the needs of a multicultural and democratic society. Puerto Rican Studies should provide real alternatives to our students, leading them toward the restructuring of the society and the relationships among its peoples. Such alternatives should be attuned to our times and the situational needs and struggles of the people. We cannot simultaneously remain an incidental supplementary curriculum in the university and also present a real alternative for self-growth and learning in the world. As Frank Bonilla once stated, we should

a. create a place where the intellectual and cultural work of our community can be performed;
b. seek to affirm and continue to explore the possibilities of collective work and new patterns of relationships in the sharing and creating of knowledge;
c. pursue the right and capacity to determine our own intellectual agenda.

Today in this conference we have taken the first step. We are assessing the problems affecting our programs and are looking into the future. This conference should result in some form of Puerto Rican Studies association. We should assess the social forces that are affecting our community, the institution, and student needs. We should start working collectively with our students and allies of our people inside and outside the university. This will entail an immediate effort to:

a. re-establish active student-teacher participation with voting rights in councils for Puerto Rican Studies;
b. elect representatives effectively accountable and subject to recall by a democratic process to such councils;
c. revamp the curriculum of Puerto Rican Studies according to the criteria established above, while seeking to positively influence the broader curriculum of the university along the same lines;
d. aggressively recruit students, even if this entails conflict over the admission policy of the university.

We are the generation responsible for the renaissance, not only of Puerto Rican Studies within the university, but also for the creation of a multicultural participatory democracy in the world. The community, the students, and the faculty must be willing and wanting to work together in a common cause. Let us seize the initiative for social change under the banner of Puerto Rican Studies as was done some ten years ago. Let us declare to the university and to the world that there is an alternative for the Puerto Rican people and for all the oppressed. *¡Vamos adelante!* (Let us move onwards!)

3
University Students as a Creative Community Force

Andrés Torres

Any discussion of the Puerto Rican student's role must initially consider the current status of our community. The following characterization will surprise no one but should be useful as a general context for our discussion.

The Puerto Rican community today is clearly in one of the most difficult phases of our history in the U.S.:

1. All socio-economic indicators demonstrate that our material reality has deteriorated both in absolute (real incomes, etc.) as well as relative (the growing gap between Puerto Rican and white incomes, etc.) terms.

2. This condition coincides with—indeed is largely determined by—the declining state of the U.S. economy and a rightward shift of the North American political spectrum. An aspect of this new political environment is the redefining of what it means to be "American." There is an obvious trend away from the idea of cultural pluralism toward the imperative of "homogenization" of the American citizen. Consequently, our community increasingly finds it necessary to adopt a basically defensive posture in order to preserve the social programs we established during the 1960s and 1970s.

3. The continual state of limbo with regard to Puerto Rico's political status has led to greater polarization and instability which has its inevitable impact on the community here in the U.S. Faced with this double presence of the "Puerto Rican problem," the U.S., as colonizing power, is at once ambivalent as well as anxious with regard to the five million Puerto Ricans on the Island and mainland. In the context of the new political con-

servatism, we can expect a hardening of U.S. attitudes to Puerto Ricans in general.

To say the least, this picture contrasts significantly with the atmosphere prevalent when Puerto Rican Studies programs were established some ten years ago. Thus, our community should not now come forth with old formulas and strategies. The role to be played by our university students will have to take into consideration these different realities.

As a general starting point, then, I would suggest that the student's role is to participate in those strategies and activities which strengthen our community's capacity to overcome its present condition. The following are steps to this end:

1. Students must see themselves as part of the historic struggle of our people for political, social, cultural, and economic *liberation*. (Further elaboration of this is invited.) This means we are talking about our students as part of a collective effort. The notion that Puerto Ricans make their most important contribution as individual models of success is pernicious because it results in the dissolution of our skills and talents. To put it in terms of a concrete example: If you *have* to work for a corporation or law firm (and there is no treachery in this!), *at least* participate directly in the affairs of our community. Experience suggests that bright young Puerto Ricans who get absorbed into institutions which don't cater to or service minorities tend to get "lost" forever; and there's plenty of space for getting lost in this country, if you want to. Recognize that without political and cultural consciousness you will not "survive" as a Puerto Rican.

2. By "community" we mean the total Puerto Rican presence. We should set aside images of poverty programs and social service institutions as the essence of our community. The Puerto Rican community, overwhelmingly working class, is to be found in factories, offices, unions, professional organizations, and an array of institutions and formations.

3. We have to distinguish between participation in the *long-run* and participation in the *short-run*. By the former we mean the acquisition of those skills which will enable the student to gain an occupation that will eventually redound to the benefit of our community. By the latter we are referring to direct involvement in our community's current struggles. We would insist that the *former* is of primary importance.

Some Problems and Obstacles

Given that we can come to some agreement on the preceding ideas, let us look at some of the principal obstacles which our students and community face and which impede a successful interaction:

1. *Confusion about students' primary role.* Our community as a whole must reinforce the importance of our students terminating their studies. Puerto Rican students—those few who have been fortunate enough to get into college—must be absolutely determined to get the maximum mileage our of their educational experience. Unfortunately, students may drop out for any number of reasons, but let it not be due to spending too much energy in community activism. There will always be time for that. However, this problem is probably not as serious as what follows.

2. *Contagious effect of the "me generation."* Not surprisingly, the very drive to succeed academically also feeds into the problem of attributing one's success strictly to one's own effort. Many students who graduate become infatuated with their own abilities and impatient with our community's situation. This is also manifest in students who spend their college years basically partying and just getting by. They have no connection with the real issues, no sense of commitment to our people. It may be true that you cannot help other people until you get your own "thing" together; but do not let this be an excuse to spend your whole lifetime in this enterprise.

3. *Elitism.* Sometimes, students contract a severe case of intellectualism; college graduates get an attitude about "professionalism." By subordinating their careers to the appearances of success and prestige, they fall into the superficiality of the "Plastic People" to whom Rubén Blades has referred.

4. *Academic Composition.* There is a reality that Puerto Rican students are overly enrolled in the areas of the social services and arts. This may be detrimental to the long-term development of our community, which also requires engineers, scientists, technicians, etc.

5. *Underdevelopment of Puerto Rican student organizations.* This occurs both at campus and regional levels; it represents a limitation to our community's development.

6. *Underdevelopment and disarticulation of our community's political strategy.* While there are ongoing efforts toward a regrouping of progressive organizations and forces, we cannot expect a clear and broad consensus to emerge overnight. This is a process

which is currently prevalent. Consequently, it creates difficulties in assessing the student's role within our community's overall strategy.

Some Directions for the Future

The preceding comments have set the stage, we hope, for the really difficult issue of coming up with practical suggestions for the future. Our objective is not simply to overcome these six (or any other) "problems." Rather it is to set out some propositions which are realistic and which, if accomplished, can serve as important stepping-stones toward the broad goal we outlined in the beginning.

1. A final appeal: stay in school! do well and get the most out of it. We need you here for now.
2. Let us begin to rebuild the Puerto Rican student movement. We need it to provide continuity and direction to the currently diffuse efforts of individual students and organizations. Such a movement should obviously focus on the immediate problems confronting students. To a large extent, the way it answers the six problems we have mentioned will determine its political frame of reference. It will have to define its principles of unity, its strategy, and a short-run program of action; also, to evolve a position on its relationship to the broader struggles of our people.
3. Puerto Rican Studies Departments should re-evaluate their programs with attention to the following questions. Can we create more linkages between university and community? Can we set up more apprenticeships or field work options with community groups? Can we possibly use work-study funds to place students in community-related projects? Can we implement real and consistent student-exchange programs with universities in Puerto Rico? Does our curriculum reflect the changing reality of the Puerto Rican experience?
4. Where possible, students and local campus organizations should get involved in the concrete struggles in which our people are engaged. Whether they be around the issue of police brutality, the threat to bi-lingual education, the need to boycott racist movies, the U.S. Navy's bombing of Vieques—whatever; these are struggles which add a real-world dimension to the educational experience. One thing is to learn of our history from books and class lectures; another is to be involved in praxis that is ideologically consistent social action.

We must critically look at our ability to accomplish these and/or other goals. In the past have we jumped into the heat of battle without knowing where we were going? Have we instinctively reacted to conditions imposed on us rather than pausing to chart out long-term perspectives?

That Puerto Rican students have a signficant role to play in our people's struggle, we take for granted. That Puerto Rican Studies can undergo a renaissance is primarily dependent on the ability of our community *in general* to grow politically, culturally, and organizationally. In turn, the strength of our community is largely influenced by the educational level and skills of our people, especially our youth. So, again, no surprise: everything is related. The question is, can be, to bring about the right blend of these elements—student, community, Puerto Rican Studies—in such a way that we make some forward motion in the struggle against oppression and for liberation? This task is only grandiose if we expect to accomplish it today; but we can at least make a beginning.

4
National and International Implications of Puerto Rican Studies: The Need for Self-Determination

By José Hernández

Major trends of social change have been classified into four main types: revolutionary, utopian, reform, regressive. In the United States, Puerto Rican Studies originated in the revolutionary and utopian thinking of the late 1960s and early 1970s. Implementation and development took shape in limited ways during a subsequent period of reform which left the existing social order essentially the same for Puerto Ricans. We assume that the United States is now in a regressive period marked by majority suspicion and distaste for changes already made and opposition to further developments in Puerto Rican Studies. As in past periods of regressive social change, avenues for stigmatization and oppression will have public approval and legitimacy. To the extent that Puerto Rican Study programs have been eliminated, curtailed, or consolidated with others, the regressive movement has already resulted in negative consequences.

How can there be a "renaissance" of Puerto Rican Studies during a period of regressive social change? Prospects for the 80–90s in some way resemble the periods subsequent to the American invasion of Puerto Rico and the ratification of the Commonwealth. In both instances a previous trend toward self-determination faced an environment in which such values as patriotism, moralism, conformity, practicality, commercial expansion, and work-for-its-own-sake prevailed over creativity, diversity, equality, freedom, leisure, challenge, and rationality. Now, as in previous instances, the colonizing pressure on Puerto Ricans will be to relinquish or substantially diminish the drive toward self-determination in favor of accomplishments considered by the dominant groups as more appropriate for the American system. Three traditional strategies for coping with regressive social changes can be summarized as follows:

"Let the regressive movement run its course." This has both active and passive forms of expression. In a regressive movement, the system's rewards will be given to Puerto Ricans showing loyalty to the conservative ideology, and penalties will be inflicted on those upholding such notions as cultural pluralism, distributive justice and self-determination. The penalties can be evaded, however, by resolving to not deliberately help in the regressive trend, and by maintaining the hope that somehow, someday things will be different. This is a strategy of negative resistance and apathy.

"Let's redirect the regressive movement through coalitions." Puerto Ricans attempting to influence social trends in the United States, on their own, have generally failed; their power in the American system is very limited. An attractive option has been to join forces with other groups having a similar experience of colonization: blacks, Chicanos, third-world people in general. To the extent that such coalitions eventually accelerate the decline of a regressive movement toward innovation and rediscovery of emancipating ideals, they may be effective in furthering the "renaissance." And experience has shown that coalitions have benefits when they include a specifically Puerto Rican agenda. When joined with the aims of other groups, our concerns and interests must be attended for coalitions to be worthwhile.

"Let's concentrate on neutral functions and activities." As a response to the adversity of the 1980s, the talent, energy, attention and resources of Puerto Rican Studies could be directed to the objectives defined by their organizational status in the university system. That is, without much regard for the prevailing social movement in the United States. This strategy asks us to perform well in services to the administration, other departments, students and the community, in general. It assumes that a quality product appeals to conservative and liberals alike— and this protects an academic program from disfavor and discontinuation. This approach may be practical to provide for the survival of Puerto Rican Studies, but it may also have limitations for their growth. A truly significant renaissance will not be a "neutral" item for most university organizations. And for the Puerto Ricans involved, the motivation must go beyond the successful fulfillment of academic duties, to create ways of expansion.

As strategies for the 1990s the approaches just outlined are only partially effective; their common weakness is their orientation to the external aspects of the Puerto Rican situation: our relation to the North American social system, to groups resembling the Puerto Rican, and the organizations in which Puerto Rican Studies are situated. Instead, we could ask ourselves the question: "What happened from inside, when a rebirth occurred in Puerto Rican culture?" In other words; "what are the conditions and attitudes that gave rise to accomplishments that were genuinely Puerto Rican, and lasting?" Detailed answers are not readily available, because the question has been seldom asked. Nevertheless, certain general observations can be made, which could be useful in creating a comprehensive agenda for the 1990s.

We know that the renaissance has generally occurred when Puerto Ricans have:

- studied and understood their own social situations
- strengthened their commitment to self-determination
- defined what people aspire to and consider important
- encouraged talented persons to pursue their aspirations and interests
- made arrangements for the expression of their efforts
- established avenues for recognition of accomplishments
- identified and coordinated resources for these purposes, from among Puerto Ricans themselves
- developed networks of people involved in furthering Puerto Rican accomplishments
- retained indigenous control over the things created.

In discussing a course of action to follow the Renaissance Conference, let us assume that the initial steps have been already taken. That is, general agreement exists on our social situation, the need for self-determination, and a renaissance of Puerto Rican Studies. Our attention could be drawn to an application of the remaining items to existing programs. Are there signs of these happening in Puerto Rican Studies? How far can each objective be developed? Ideas for growth in Puerto Rican Studies could emerge from answers to such questions, as responded by experts and participants.

By avoiding exclusive reliance on negative resistance and apathy, coalitions, and neutral academic functions, chances are that Puerto Rican Studies would have the freedom and energy to evolve an effective strategy for going beyond survival to a renaissance—despite the regressive social change movement in the United States. A critical examination of factors contributing to self-determination and past accomplishments in Puerto Rican culture will serve to give substance to the agenda to be developed. If given momentum, the agenda for the 1990s will succeed and what has happened during similar periods of the past need not be repeated.

PART TWO

THE CURRICULUM OF
PUERTO RICAN STUDIES

5
Puerto Rican Studies and Bilingual Education

Sonia Nieto

In order to consider bilingual education as a curriculum area within Puerto Rican Studies a working definition would be useful. I suggest bilingual education be defined as "those insights, methods, and competencies which prepare students to become teachers committed to the liberation of Puerto Rican and other Third World children and youth." The focus of this defintion is on the process of teaching rather than on the content of bilingual education. That is, it is a primarily political focus. This is not to imply that issues of language, materials, and curriculum are unimportant; rather, it is to suggest that these issues must be viewed within a political perspective.

A typical school of education usually has the resources necessary for teacher training and in fact often does a creditable job of supplying the market with teachers. But although they may be using the latest methods, technology, and competencies, the perspective unique to Puerto Rican Studies is often lost under such limited confines.

Bilingual education has not been addressed by all Puerto Rican Studies departments as a curriculum area. This is unfortunate because bilingual education probably affects our lives as profoundly or more so than other curriculum areas to which we Puerto Ricans have dedicated our time. In concrete terms, teachers educated with a Puerto Rican Studies perspective would potentially have a greater impact on our bilingual communities.

Given the interdisciplinary nature of Puerto Rican Studies, it would seem to make sense to unite in some fashion these two perspectives, joining a philosophical and political awareness to the acquisition of concrete educational skills. At some universities this kind of marriage has been in place for years. Often, it has suffered from both petty squabbles and major disagreements; sometimes, divorce has been contemplated. Yet it is still the best way to ensure the complete education of our "teachers/students." This term, coined by Paulo Freire, indicates the reciprocity of teaching and learning. That is, students are often teachers and teachers are often students. I believe this is a particularly useful way of viewing students of Puerto Rican Studies in bilingual education for it emphasizes the active, analytical, and liberating aspects of pedagogy.

A second focus is one which has permeated all curriculum areas in Puerto Rican Studies: field-based practical experiences to augment abstract, theoretical knowledge. Praxis is especially crucial in education where instruction programs with this focus have consistently been the most successful.

A model core curriculum in bilingual education built upon these foundations might include more or all of the following:

- Philosophy of Bilingual Education
- Issues in Linguistics for the Puerto Rican Community
- Puerto Rican Children in the United States
- Community Organizing for Bilingual Education
- Curriculum Development for Bilingual Classrooms
- Teaching Spanish Language Arts
- Second Language Acquisition
- Methods and Materials in Content Areas
- Education for Liberation: Experience in Other Countries
- The Role of Puerto Rican History and Culture in Bilingual Classrooms
- Multilingual and Ethnic Education in a Pluralistic Society
- Research Methods in Bilingual Education
- Observations and Student Teaching in Bilingual Classrooms.

Not all of these experiences must, or indeed should, be completed courses. Depending on the needs and resources of the particular program there could be workshops, seminars, or modules lasting anywhere from several hours to several weeks. These would supplement the traditional courses. The variety of experiences would allow for a more flexible, student-oriented program. In addition, seminars centering on particular issues of concern could be offered as the need arose.

The problems generally associated with a bilingual education component within a Department of Puerto Rican Studies have been:

a. An overwhelming reliance, both on the part of students and outside faculty, on the Department of Puerto Rican Studies to meet most of the academic and other needs of its students.
b. A lack of solid research on the Puerto Rican community in the United States upon which to base our program.
c. A tendency of both students and faculty to remain isolated from the mainstream of bilingual education.

Each of these must be described more fully along with possible directions for the future.

After ten years of experience, it is time to reconceptualize the role of bilingual education within Puerto Rican Studies. All of the following recommendations center on expansion beyond the traditional limits. I believe this broadening of our traditional perspective can be described as "networking."

a. Expanding our Frontiers: Working with the University-at-Large

Our first question must be: what are the responsibilities of other departments within the university of our students? In other words, what competencies for bilingual education as well as general knowledge can other departments help to foster? Clearly, no Puerto Rican Studies curriculum can hope to cover all areas adequately. It is time to reach out to other programs, departments, and schools within our universities to demand that they too fulfill their responsibilities to our students. Until now, we have been expected to provide for every need of our students, a task which we are neither capable of, nor have the resources to, carry out.

b. Research: A New Priority

The past ten years for Puerto Rican Studies have been about organization and survival. It is now time to go beyond that. With the institutionalization of bilingual education, the priority in the coming years will be research. Yet most research in bilingual education does not focus on issues of concern of the Puerto Rican community. This is so for several reasons, not the least of which is the fact that even when research centering on the Puerto Rican community is undertaken, it is generally carried out by non-Puerto Ricans. Our particular perspective as well as our reality is missing from research on bilingual education. Policy decisions based on so-called Puerto Rican research ignores the experiences of Puerto Ricans. The excellent work of the Center for Puerto Rican Studies at CUNY which developed a linguistic policy based on research of and for the Puerto Rican community is a model for all Puerto Rican Studies Departments. Another organization to which we can turn is the Puerto Rican Migration Research Consortium. Collaborative efforts with agencies or groups such as these may help individual programs of Puerto Rican Studies to strengthen the practical aspects of bilingual education by strengthening our theoretical base.

c. Widening the Perspective: Working with Local, State, and National Organizations

The lack of progressive voices in bilingual education is embarrassing. Given the roots of bilingual education, it is also a disgrace. Yet, how many faculty or students from departments of Puerto Rican Studies are in organizatioins like NABE, PREA, and SABE? (How many even know what they stand for?) How many are on advisory councils for bilingual education? How many work with or run for office on local school boards? Often, those of us in Puerto Rican Studies have remained on the fringes of the bilingual education establishment. Whether this has been a result of our insularism or of our discomfort in associating so closely with traditional educators is a moot point. The outcome has been to isolate bilingual education from serious political analysis. How many persons in bilingual education, for example, still see it as a panacea to all our ills? How many still believe in the "culture of poverty?" How many accept the notion that bilingual education is compensatory education? Why are they, in fact, teachers: Are they out to "save" our children with the zeal of missionaires before them? Or are they there to bring out the contradictions of the educational system, to bring about change and liberation? The contribution of Puerto Rican Studies, particularly an understanding of education as a political process, must begin to make itself felt on all levels of the bilingual education movement.

d. Further Questions for Study

I must confess that there are other issues which impact directly on bilingual education within a Puerto Rican Studies perspective which I have not even brought up. Yet they are serious questions which deserve serious analysis. To that end I will list them here for further consideration and study:

1. By placing bilingual education programs within Departments of Puerto Rican Studies, are we not in fact claiming this area as the "turf" of solely the Puerto Rican community? What about the concerns of communities such as the Chinese, Italian, Korean and Greek, not to mention other Caribbean and Latin people? My concern here is

that we may be further alienating some natural or at least potential allies by concentrating our efforts and our curriculum solely on the Puerto Rican community.

2. By focusing on bilingual teacher education, I have completely neglected the role of what has been called a "Bilingual Mini-College" or "Bilingual Studies" at various colleges. These programs offer students academic courses in their native language while they learn English. Several questions arise: Can, or should, a Puerto Rican Studies Department sponsor this type of program? With what resources? Should this program require any minimum proficiency in English prior to graduation? How could it be done? And if it is not done, are we not in fact condemning our graduates to failure if they cannot function without some minimal skills in English?

3. Bilingual education within Puerto Rican Studies has focused only on the Puerto Rican community. This has been based on several factors. One is that most of our students were prepared to work in Puerto Rican communities. Another is that a connection has to be made between bilingual education and an aggressive cultural statement. Now, however, this may be changing somewhat and we must ask ourselves: what are the new frontiers in multilingual, multicultural education, and how can we use them? And if we do indeed include them in our perspective bilingual education, will we be violating our own commitment to preparing teachers who are intimately aware of the linguistic, cultural, and political realities of Puerto Rican children? These concerns merit serious study if we are to meet the challenge of survival in the years ahead.

Based on the foregoing comments, I would make these recommendations:

(a) We ought to begin consultation with university-wide representatives to explore the possibility of meaningful collaboration between Puerto Rican Studies Departments and other departments, programs, and schools. Students and faculty from all departments involved would be represented.

(b) We would develop a "Student" Research Center for Puerto Rican Studies, funded by CUNY, to which both undergraduate and graduate students could apply for financial support to carry out research. The governing board of the center, made up of students and faculty from all the CUNY campuses, would make final decisions on awarding contracts based on resources and priorities. In addition, staff at the Center for Puerto Rican Studies would be available to provide technical assistance in carrying out research projects. Housing this new center within the Center for Puerto Rican Studies at CUNY would probably be a sensible decision.

(c) We would set up formal linkages with agencies and organizations serving the Puerto Rican community for purposes of both research and practicum experiences. These might vary from professional associations such as PREA to community groups such as the United Bronx Parents, and of course, to local school boards.

In defining bilingual education as a potentially liberating force, I would like to cite Paulo Freire: "Every educational practice implies a concept of man and the world."[1] Thus, bilingual education is more than an educational practice; it is also a vision for the transformation of our students at the university and, in turn, for our children. Given the directions for the future I've described, it is possible that each student would have different experiences, almost an individualized curriculum based on individual interests and talents. An example of a typical student's program within this untypical curriculum might be:

- A semester-long course on the "Philosophy of Bilingual Education" culminating in a statements of objectives for bilingual education for the Puerto Rican community.
- Two weekend seminars on "Education for Liberation: The South American Experiences" taught by a visiting scholar from Nicaragua, so that students can see the revolutionary dimensions of education.
- A research project focusing on the use of Spanish among Kindergarten children, for credit in the Linguistics Department.
- A year long practicum on "Community Organizing for Bilingual Education" at the Puerto Rican Legal Defense and Education Fund.
- A "Spanish Language Arts" course taught by a Puerto Rican Studies Department with a practicum in a day-care center.
- A literacy project for adults in conjunction with a course on curriculum development, co-sponsored by the Spanish or Romance Language Department.
- A year's internship working on the editorial board of the publication of the Puerto Rican Educators' Association in conjunction with the College Journalism Program.
- A curriculum development project on Puerto Rican Women for the high school level, co-sponsored by the Women's Studies Program.

Some of these options may sound unrealistic, others impossible. Yet it will only be through expanding our horizons that Puerto Rican Studies will make an impact on the university, the community, and the nation, areas which all too often have either ignored or neglected our presence. It is time to make our presence felt.

Notes

1. See Paolo Freire, "Cultural Action for Freedom," in *Education for Critical Consciousness.* New York: Seabury Press, 1973.

6
Puerto Rican Studies and Latin American History

Loida Figueroa Mercado

It is imperative to visualize the revitalization and re-evaluation of future courses of study within the major cultural compass of Latin America in which Puerto Rico plays a part. It cannot escape our consideration that researchers and scholars in our academic community have been somewhat estranged from the general Latin American cultural milieu. While it would be overly ambitious to try to reconstruct and re-integrate the whole of this vast area of study, a reunion of one segment, the history of the Caribbean nations of Latin America and Puerto Rico is proposed. To be successful, the approach to this juncture must necessarily be gradual and systematic.

As the first step in the approach toward the integration of Latin American/Puerto Rican Studies, we propose a concentration in the area of the Hispanic Caribbean, Puerto Rico, Cuba, and the Dominican Republic, followed by an extension to the non-Hispanic Caribbean. A further progression to the historical relationship of the Caribbean nations and Central America, Yucatán, and the countries bordering the Caribbean Sea to the south, Columbia and Venezuela, completes the survey. The course contains the following topics:

First: An overall spectrum of the Hispanic Caribbean should begin with the following:

a. The general characteristics of the Spanish conquest and their effects upon the cultures of the Caribbean.

b. If possible, attention should be given to the original African cultures in their native continent. Proper emphasis should be given to the impact of these involuntary invaders on the economics and the formation of the new Caribbean nationalities.

c. The devélopment of the new nationalities based on the mixture of races and cultures, with their subsequent struggles for independence from the colonial powers. Special consideration is required in the case of the Dominican Republic since it was once under the domination of another American nation, Haiti.

Moreover, the study of the Hispanic nations of the West Indian Archipelago should build on the following common experiences.

1. The term "Hispanic" is used for purposes of differentiation based on the historical factor of the Spanish conquest of these nations and its subsequent cultural domination. This does not mean that the other components of our cultural heritage are to be ignored. Precisely what Cuba, the Dominican Republic, and Puerto Rico have in common is the pre-Columbian substratum, in particular, the Arawak culture, and the African influences added to the West Indian fabric by the slaves brought from across the ocean.

2. Ever since the European conquests, the two Americas were given the role of providers of raw materials produced by slave and/ or cheap free labor. Thus began the hemispheric division of labor which separated the continents into two blocs—the industrialized or "developed nations," and the agricultural or "underdeveloped nations." The Caribbean nations included in the proposed study fall into the second and larger category. Consequently, in any course on the area, proper emphasis must be given to the economic history and present day structure of the region within a capitalistic framework and especially in relation to the neighboring United States. Here a wide range of historical analysis can be extracted based on dependence and development theories, the importation of capital intensive industry and the exportation of surplus labor, and the effects of industrialization and modernization in the Caribbean.

3. The Hispanic nations of the Caribbean represent three types of politico-economic systems. Puerto Rico remains today the classic colonial possession, in spite of modifications and euphemisms. The Dominican Republic, although an independent nation, operates under close surveillance and threatened intervention by the United States. Cuba represents the first socialist country in the Americas. The relationship and interdependence among these three distinct political types and the other nations bordering the Caribbean emerges as a critical area of study, particularly at a time when the contest between

the dominant political systems of the western hemisphere are being
put to a test.

Although I could have included a bibliography of secondary and
primary sources available in the libraries of Puerto Rico, the bulk of
relevant materials must be pursued in New York City since Puerto
Rican Studies is heavily concentrated there. I would call attention to
a set of documents housed in the archives of the Institute of Puerto
Rican Studies at Brooklyn College related to the impact of the
multinationals in the Dominican Republic. Besides scouting the New
York Public Library on Fifth Avenue, research should be conducted
in the Schomberg Collection if proper attention is given to the African
contributions in Caribbean cultures. Other sources could be the
embassies or consulates of Caribbean countries in New York City,
and the United Nations Cuban Mission in the United States. Finally,
the establishment of contacts with the universities of Caribbean
nations, particularly the Hispanic Caribbean must be initiated and
maintained. The Institute of Caribbean Studies and the Norte-Sur
Center in Puerto Rico are two such examples. It is precisely in these
settings where efforts at joint or integrated research can begin, healing
in the process, the rupture between those academics dedicated to the
study of Latin America and those in the area of Puerto Rican Studies.
Major resistance to this proposed new direction in the integration
of Latin American Puerto Rican Studies might be forthcoming from
other university departments which include related courses. Traditional
departments have jealously guarded their disciplines failing to acknowledge the academic accomplishments and contributions of less
traditional, interdisciplinary units. Indeed, the study of Latin America
and the Caribbean has often been relegated less importance in relation
to United States and European history. It is ironic that this attitude
still exists in spite of the growing numbers of Hispanic and third
world students entering urban universities today.
A second problem is the lack of an inclusive text for such a course.
On the Mayagüez campus, for example, a course on the History of
the West Indies appears in the catalogue but neither the course as
designed nor the texts used cover the economic content or the
comparative nature as proposed for the integrated course. The instructors for a course on Latin American/Caribbean/Puerto Rican
Studies must be aware of the most recent scholarship in the fields.
They will have to use a variety of materials and the compilation of
a series of readings into a usable basic reader might serve as a feasible
alternative.

To supplement the readings I stress once again, articulation with the universities of Cuba, the Dominican Republic, and Puerto Rico. Perhaps the establishment of a systematic network composed of specialists in these areas could lead to the sharing of occasional papers, visiting lecturers, and exchanges among the faculties of the respective institutions. Lecturers could be invited to speak and deliver up-to-date information on specific themes, and if the instructors of the proposed course are able to spend summers attending seminars or engaged in serious research at Caribbean universities, the results would be fruitful for all concerned.

Moreover, it would be desirable if the students who matriculate for the proposed course have some previous knowledge of the history, politics, and economics of Puerto Rico as well as a fair awareness of international economic history. It goes without saying that such students would also benefit greatly from a summer or semester of study abroad. Seminars which provide these opportunities would serve as natural extensions of the proposed course.

The 1980s may well witness a substantial change in the political status of Puerto Rico. Hence, thought should be given to the consequences of such changes for Puerto Rican Studies within the structure of the City University of New York. What must be remembered is that if Puerto Rico becomes independent, many Puerto Ricans will choose to stay in the United States. This decision will necessitate the continuity of Puerto Rican Studies. As students, faculty, and community supporters demanded the creation of Puerto Rican and Ethnic Studies in the past, today's students will require even stronger ties with an independent Puerto Rico. On the other hand, statehood as a political alternative poses the threat of complete assimilation within the dominant United States culture. It is up to the leaders of the Puerto Rican communities in the States and to the Departments of Puerto Rican Studies to insure the continuity of academic and community services within or outside the City University. Now is the time to strengthen those colleges with large concentrations of Puerto Ricans who do not wish to lose their cultural identity nor sever their ties with the Latin American world. Regardless of how the status issue is resolved, Puerto Ricans in the United States must be served.

In order to put the course outlined in this paper into motion, solicitation of funds should be made for the time being among the private foundations in existence in the United States, particularly in view of government retrenchment in public funding. This would allow the planning and financing of feasible trips and research by professors and students in the Caribbean islands. It would also compensate the visits of eminent lecturers from Caribbean universities to New York

City. We must consider the creation of a committee of specialists in the proposed fields of study to oversee this phase of the plan. This will set the pace for the long-range purposes suggested beforehand.

Taking the first step to integrate Latin American, Caribbean, and Puerto Rican Studies will contribute to the agenda of the Department of Puerto Rican Studies "to articulate our concerns to a wider national and international audience." If the objectives of the course are attained, the Puerto Rican community, particularly through the influence of our students and teachers, will have a wider outlook and a clear vision of their past contributions and future role in the history of the Americas.

7

Puerto Rican Studies and Ethnic/Black Studies: Current Problems and Future Strategies

Jesse M. Vázquez

This paper proposes to focus on the broader issues affecting curriculum development in Puerto Rican Studies, by surveying the general problems, limitations, ideological considerations and strategies in developing a meaningful curriculum for Puerto Rican Studies. Our general analytical framework for this discussion should allow those involved in other ethnic studies programs the opportunity to draw from their own experiences and thereby make cross-programmatic comparisons. In effect, what are the issues which are commonly shared by other ethnic studies programs and what might these common themes teach us by closely examining the problems inherent in developing a core or generalized curriculum for Puerto Rican Studies? For purposes of this paper we will define curriculum in its broadest terms to include a series or an aggregate of courses of study in a given program or department concerned with the Puerto Rican or other ethnic group's experience.

This presentation will focus on a number of basic and practical issues which seem to be commonly shared by all those who find themselves responsible for developing the general direction of the overall curriculum for an ethnic studies program. We will not deal with specific subject matter areas. We will, however, explore those underlying dynamics and factors which generally tend to have an impact on each of the subject areas, and ultimately shape the form and substance of an ethnic studies program or department.

These problems and issues briefly stated include the following:

1. Fundamental purpose of a Puerto Rican or other ethnic studies curriculum
2. Bureaucratic and territorial concerns in curriculum development
3. Enrollment figures and their impact on curriculum
4. Texts and other materials used in our curriculum
5. Who do we select to teach our curriculum?

Major Problem Areas

First: One must ask what is it that we want to teach? Why teach a particular course at all? What might be its purpose within the larger scheme of the community and the society? Perhaps some may consider this concern to come under the well worn banner of "relevance," but my question suggests a deeper more fundamental concern. (The notion of relevance, made popular during the 1960s, has become a code word in traditionalist academia for courses with little content and resulting in easy A's.) My concern, therefore, is not so much with popular and distorted notion of relevance, but with the meaning that a curriculum might have in assuring the continuity and survival of a people and of a culture in contemporary American society.

In developing curriculum we should constantly be mindful of the fact that a scant ten years ago most of us were actively struggling to carve out a place and a space in the university. We are here today teaching about our culture and political realities because of our continued struggle to survive in the university as we struggle to survive in the larger society. So in a very real sense our pedagogical questions—of what to teach—must be placed within the larger social context of who and what we represent in the society at large. Sometimes in our zeal to develop courses for our programs, we lose sight of why we are here at all. Why the university?

When one looks back at the student struggles which gave rise to the departments and programs of Puerto Rican and other ethnic studies, we find very little that provides a recommended series of courses or even guidelines for a core curriculum. There was, however, an underlying common ideological and pedagogical base. Today after ten years of experimentation it seems that we have lost sight of some of those founding principles. And this will of necessity reflect itself in the form and substance of our curriculum. However, if our political and economic conditions have altered our reality in the university, should we not seriously examine some of the guiding or founding principles which brought us here in the first place? If our curriculum or our programs are victims of cultural lag, ought we not submit our programs, and especially our curriculum, to meticulous scrutiny?

So one issue, and perhaps the most critical and fundamental issue that is a significant force in shaping our curriculum today, springs from the very basic ideological principles which carried us *en masse* into the university ten years ago. Are these principles still valid? I shall elaborate on this question in the final section.

Second: In developing a single course or indeed an entire coherent curriculum, we must work within, around, and through the bureaucratic limitations imposed upon us by each academic entity. Here we face the issue of "turf" or "academic territoriality." We are the newcomers, the academic interlopers crossing over into other disciplines, and threatening the sacred boundaries of the traditional academic departments. At Queens College, for example, a number of program directors have huddled together in an effort to protect our ethnic studies curriculum against departmental assault. This self-protective band is called the Ethnic Studies Council.[1] This council, however tenuous, does provide a sense of common purpose, direction and coordination of ethnic studies courses. We recognize daily that the issue of turf will continue to be a very real obstacle to the potential development of most ethnic studies programs. This resistance will become more heated as resources and student enrollment continues to shrink in the coming decades. We can anticipate a stepped-up interest in ethnic studies coming from those traditional departments as they begin to experience significant declines in their own enrollment figures. Naturally, they will seek to recapture students and will begin by challenging our right to teach particular courses which they perceive to "rightfully" belong in their bailiwick. Obviously, each program finds itself in a marginal subculture of the academic community, but each of us must continue to stress and make use of the interdisciplinary approach or method. Recognizing the vulnerability of this position in the academy, I view the interdisciplinary method as possibly the only sensible way to approach the study of the Puerto Rican or other ethnic groups in contemporary society. To allow our studies to be coopted by distinctive academic departments would not make sense in terms of preserving scholarly academic consistency, and certainly would contradict our basic insistence on creating an autonomous academic entity in the university.

Third: A quite fundamental issue which has a direct impact on our curriculum is enrollment—the "numbers game." Enrollment figures are tied directly to the life or death of a course, and eventually could have a profound impact on an entire program. Our desire to guarantee high enrollment in our courses may at times cause us to lose sight of quality and meaningfulness in our curriculum. Popular courses may produce high figures, but at the same time they may be moving the programs away from our fundamental goals and concerns. If pushing courses is a phenomenon that is also accompanied by a dilution of the program's central focus or thrust, then students and faculty must examine what is happening on that particular campus. For example, we must determine the extent to which we have drifted from some of the founding goals of Puerto Rican Studies. In effect, our market place response to our curriculum offerings can be the first clear sign that something is critically wrong with the program and its faculty. And perhaps a lack of student awareness of our intended goals is also a warning that something has gone astray. Of course, we cannot deny the fact that some courses are extremely popular with the students and are also fundamental to the study of the Puerto Rican or other ethnic group's experience.

Our enrollment problems, if we have any, are key to the survival of any program or department. The question we must address is, how do we respond to these pressures for increased enrollment, and how do these demands reshape the content and form of our curriculum offerings?

Fourth: An area which naturally has a significant impact on our curriculum and its content is the substance and quality of our course materials and texts. I will not probe the specific subject areas in this discussion because other speakers and panels are dealing with their own specializations. I want to address some of the general concerns in an attempt to focus on how the quality of texts and materials can either enhance or significantly reduce the impact of our curriculum.

In selecting texts, articles, and other reading materials, we are first and foremost faced with the question of what sources would be most suitable for our particular course. What then are the criteria which determine "suitability" or "appropriateness" of the selected reading material? One key determinant would be to use the course level as a guide. Another area of concern would be to determine who your students are, and what their academic skills and deficiencies might be. Should we require one main text or assign additional readings on reserve? Do our students make use of the reserve reading materials? If not, why not? How many of us have not seriously considered the costs of texts and financial burden on the students? Knowing that many of our students are poor, may prohibit us from assigning a long list of required books for one course.

Beyond these concerns, many of us have found the book or text market quite inappropriate for our purposes. And because of this situation, many of our instructors have certainly stretched the bounds and limits of the new copyright laws. Instructors, over the years, have gathered significant collections of excellent journal articles as well a newspaper clippings which may serve as an excellent source for course material. Many of us have sought to formalize and have organized these collections into one bound volume for classroom use. This method has been particularly useful in the area of new or experimental courses which may not become a part of the core curriculum. For example, last year in cooperation with a visiting professor, our program put together a specialized text for a course title, *Natural Resources and Environmental Issues in Puerto Rico* (Prof. Neftali Garcia-Martinez, Queens College 1980). There was no text for this kind of course, so the instructor had to create it with his own published material.

Another area of concern, which I shall just mention in passing, is the issue of language of the text or article. Some materials are exclusively printed in Spanish, others are in English, and others are available in both. Selecting the reading language for a particular course is a critical question which is tied to the purpose of the course content and its goals. What are the specific subject areas involved? What are our expectations for our students in these areas? Again, this question will probably be part of the discussion of the subject matter workshops; however, this issue is of crucial importance in the development of meaningful coherent Puerto Rican Studies curriculum.

While we see ample evidence of creative use and transformation of resource material, we should seek to explore a more consistent means of developing and disseminating these kinds of materials. After all, the success or failure of any learning experience rests heavily on the kinds of reading materials used in that particular course or program. An innovative curriculum in Puerto Rican Studies or any ethnic studies program must be supported by a creative well thought out and balanced selection fo reading resources, which should include print as well as non-print material.

Fifth: A concern which has a most direct impact on our curriculum is the question of who teaches our courses—instructional staff. Historically, we have found that our criteria for selecting and maintaining instructors for Puerto Rican Studies have deviated dramatically from those established by the university. Where we have stressed commitment and knowledge of the Puerto Rican community and specifically knowledge of the subject area, the university has demanded credentials. They want to see the Ph.D. This notion persists today more than ever. We have seen our largest programs stripped of young innovative instructors for want of their doctoral degree. So-called uncredentialed faculty are maintained on adjunct lecturer lines, or in other cases are released (fired) before they are awarded their lecturer's tenure. In fact, because of these destructive regressive policies, we have seen the creation and emergence of a class of migrant adjunct lecturers within the CUNY system and other private institutions. Some chairpersons have succumbed to the demands for the Ph.D. requirements in ways that only have served to hurt young committed and creative instructors.

If we are going to maintain control over what is taught through our curriculum, we must continue to struggle to maintain control over who teaches our courses. I am not naive enough to think that this is an easy task. It is not. Frank Bonilla and Emilio Gonzalez in an article written almost ten years ago strongly suggested that:

> (f) Puerto Ricans cannot rely exclusively on the academically certified or scientifically trained in pursuit of the kind of self-knowledge we seek. We must build toward excellence, but put to work the talent we have at every stage of growth.[2]

Experience has taught us that the instructor's ability to transmit the essence of the material is our program's primary responsibility. The ability to convey a message and a sense of urgency and relevance attached to the material only comes from an individual who has a broader and deeper sense of why he or she is teaching in a Puerto Rican Studies program and not in sociology, history, or economics department. Our curriculum is made to come alive and real by an instructor who is committed to a concept of teaching and learning which promotes scholarship as well as social and community involvement. Instructors should present a curriculum that seeks to explore the theoretical dimensions of particular issues and problems in the community, as well as to explore the potential for social and political change.

The critical connection between the quality of curriculum and who teaches in our programs is self-evident. However, what may be more subtle, and not as direct, is how and who we choose to teach our courses. The danger lies in submitting to the traditionalist's sole criterion for excellence—the Ph.D.

Directions for the Future

The many issues affecting curriculum and ultimately the future of Puerto Rican and other ethnic studies programs suggests the obvious: that is, that we are engaged in a perpetual struggle to retain a place within the university. If we find one day that magically our curriculum has been fully accepted by traditional departments without any struggle, we can assume that either the university has been transformed or that a diluted ineffectual series of courses dealing with the Puerto Rican experience has been accepted. On the other hand, we may also find that we have indeed learned something about academia and how it could be made to work for our own ethnic community. Therefore, given the current trends and conditions in higher education, how might we proceed and what should we be mindful of in the coming decade?[3]

First: It should be noted that academic bureaucratic warfare has required much social and psychological energy and concentration. While we have been kept busy demonstrating that our programs and departments are viable academic entities, we have experienced a systematic depletion of our numbers and resources on campuses throughout CUNY and other institutions. This simply means that we will begin to see an increasing number of our courses taught by part-time personnel. This trend will have a calamitous impact on our programs as our numbers continue to decline in the university. We all know that the university uses adjuncts to cut costs. But we also know that consistency and excellence in curriculum can come only from a faculty that feels and experiences options for permanency and promotion beyond the semester to semester contracts given to adjuncts. I can state without hesitation that most of the adjunct instructors I have worked with in Puerto Rican Studies have demonstrated a commitment that far exceeds their contractual obligations. They have demonstrated a deep sense of commitment to their students, the program, and to the community. Some kind of action must be taken to reverse the trend toward relying on part time instructors.

Second: Recognizing our problems in the availability of useful texts and materials, future efforts should be directed toward the publication of resource materials especially designed for our courses. There are unique problems in this area, and it seems that we might benefit from exploring the feasibility of establishing our own publishing organization. This capability would serve us in a variety of areas. Its main focus, however, would be to print and disseminate materials for Puerto Rican Studies.

I might add, parenthetically, that our efforts at publication and dissemination have been somewhat uneven and lacking some degree of consistency. We have seen far too many good journals come and go much too frequently. Many of you, I am certain, will recall *The Rican's* impact on our community at the particular time. And currently, the "working papers" published by El Centro are widely distributed and are accepted as important and significant pieces of research. However, the problem here is that research institutes are funded primarily to do research. And the publication of the research, at least for larger audiences, is a costly and time consuming process. What we need is a group whose primary focus is the publication of materials and the reprinting of valuable materials that are out of print. And today, as long as the agenda calls for long-range strategies, we should seriously consider the formation of such a publishing house supported by scholarly and community organizations.

Third: My expressed concern over enrollment and its critical impact on curriculum is an issue requiring serious examination. We know, for example, that there are many complex factors which have a direct and indirect bearing on the numbers of students registering or not registering for courses. These variables include, among others, the following:

- hour and day of the week course is scheduled
- instructor's reputation
- number of course requirements (exams, papers, etc.)
- students' perception of the importance of that particular course in the larger scheme of his/her life in the community or in academia
- publicity given a course or lack of it.

These variables, and many others not mentioned, have at one time or another combined to close down a course before the first week of class. I mention these factors because they have a direct impact on what a program or department will offer as part of its schedule for a particular semester. And if we go about this task with only numbers in mind, then we might be consigning our programs to a rather gloomy and pointless future.

In connection with this question, we must know how our students perceive our curriculum and what it means to them. Those students who enter the university today see only that our Puerto Rican Studies programs are in place. They perceive us as a fixed and immutable part of the institution. We're in the bulletin, we have an office with our name on the door, our courses are listed in the schedule, instructors post office hours, we have office personnel to answer questions, etc., etc. All those symbols give the illusion of permanency. What they do not see is the historical struggle that brought us there in the first place. And, furthermore, there is a failure (perhaps our own) to recognize that our programs and departments are constantly on the brink of total dissolution. It is up to us to close the gap between the perceived illusion of legitimacy and the political reality which threatens to eliminate our programs. So it becomes critical for us to educate our students to this institutional reality and conflict. We must clearly state that our curriculum is simply not a matter of a Puerto Rican scholar offering a disconnected sociology, psychology, or political science course, but that our efforts seek to go beyond the pedagogical boundaries of theoretical discussion.

If our courses are in danger, then our students must be told of this danger, and understand what it is that the curriculum, the program, and our presence in the university represents. So when we play the "numbers game," we ought to remain vigilant and know consciously that our efforts to get greater enrollment, to satisfy the funding formulae, may conflict with our reasons for being in the university in the first place.

Fourth: In noting the impact of the academic bureaucracy and departmental territoriality on the development and shaping of our curriculum, I suggested that as budgets tighten up we will begin to experience an ever-increasing level of protest from our colleagues in the established disciplines. I am certain that we have already seen evidence of this trend in our own institutions. At the same time, we should not be deceived by a rekindling of interest in ethnic studies coming from these same departments. We are seen as competitors in the student enrollment market. These departments will, as they have in the past, restate their right to offer ethnic studies courses, and that ethnic studies courses should be offered exclusively through their anointed and established departments. As Professor Orlando Patterson from Harvard, in talking about the future of Black Studies, stated:

> We strongly suspect that many . . . programs across the country are poised on the edge. If money is tight and enrollments are declining and politically things are quiet, this would be the right time (for their opponents) to close them.[4]

It is obvious that our academic marginality reflects our economic and social marginality. So given these conditions of scarcity in the academic market place, we must approach the task of curriculum design with a clarity of purpose which reflects the community's reasons for being in the university. No doubt the question of departmental hegemony over ethnic studies is complicated by the faculty's need for security and academic anchoring in a home department. In fact, the question of where ethnic studies instructional faculty are housed, has become an issue which has affected many department and programs throughout the country. The intricate connections between where faculty is housed or who has the right or franchise for offering a particular course, or the issue of crossing over sensitive discipline boundaries in an interdisciplinary course, all contribute to sustaining a atmosphere of challenge and distrust. And, of course, ethnic studies curriculum is always guaranteed a challenge from most quarters of the academic community. How many of us have had to respond to the questions which I believe pointedly express the establishment's disdain for our very presence in the university; "Do you really think that there is a body of literature to justify an entire semester of work for a course like that?"

These questions and presumptions from within the academic community should serve not only to sharpen our survival skills in the academy, but should also push us toward a clearer definition of what it is that we want to teach and where exactly do we want to go with our curriculum.

Finally, allow me to go back to my first concern and how it affects the curriculum. That concern focuses on why we are here at all. Why have we selected the univesity as another arena for community struggle? Are we here to offer a standardized well-balanced core curriculum? I don't think so, or at least not exclusively are we here for that purpose. Are we here then to guarantee employment for scholars seeking legitimization from the academic establishment? I think not, although sometimes our need for financial security and need for individual recognition does seem to place these concerns above others. Or perhaps, are we here to round out our student's schedules with a conveniently timed course? Again, I would hope that we as a community of students and faculty have not become that removed from the struggles of our people.

My sense is that many of us have gotten lost along the way, and that our need for survival as academic entities has eclipsed our focus and reason for being in the university in the first place. We all know from our experience that there are many ways of surviving "on the street." Some paths, as we know, lead to a slow painful death and other roads lead to a toughening of the spirit, and this in turn leads to a greater commitment of self to the community.

What we teach in our curriculum or through it, should be in direct response to our original purposes for being in the university. I am not so certain that the essential reasons and purposes have changed in the last ten years. But it seems to me that the social and economic conditions of our people have deteriorated significantly in the last decade as amply demonstrated by the latest statistical reports. And then, of course, our own observations of our conditions here and in Puerto Rico, support this conclusion. Yet, I wonder why these observations and conclusions have not been directly expressed in our activities on a political level, or indeed on social and educational fronts? And, in particular, why these conditions have not translated themselves into active advocacy positions in our program activities and curriculum? I am sure we could all speculate as to why we have entered such a period of political malaise. We have witnessed a kind of somnolence take hold of us. Some of you may recall our initial efforts last year to build a Puerto Rican Council for Higher Education. Welcomed with enthusiastic support at the beginning, the Council slowly faded out toward the end of the academic year. It died because a handful of faculty involved could not carry the load for Puerto Ricans in all of the CUNY units. Why do we find it so difficult at this time to act in our own behalf?

These comments are not intended as a condemnation of our work, for we are all aware that we have made some significant advances in the structure. But these efforts and our directions have been somewhat fragmented. Our vision of Puerto Rican Studies curriculum today in many instances has been the byproduct of our need to accommodate. In these ten years, in many ways, we have isolated ourselves from one another. And in this isolation we might have become provincial and somewhat parochial. However, now we suddenly have discovered that in our zeal to secure a "legitimate" place in the academy, we realize that we may have compromised some of our initial goals and principles.

If we review all of the problems and issues which have had a significant impact on the shape and content of the curriculum in Puerto Rican and other ethnic studies programs, we can generally conclude that we can and we have indeed learned to deal with and negotiate the intricacies of the academic system. We also know that we have had an intensive experience in formulating strategies to cope with budget cuts and reduction of faculty. And in some instances, we can and have formed collective action around the issues of scholarly publications and have developed our own course material. And, furthermore, each of us has had to confront intransigent traditionalist undergraduate curriculum committees to justify the validity of our courses. While I suggest that these are critical issues requiring our immediate concentrated attention, we must, nevertheless, answer a more fundamental question. What is it that we are doing in the university—and what is it that we want our curriculum to convey to our students and to our community? My sense is that we should at least re-examine some of these founding principles and purposes. And in so doing, determine the extent to which we have made practical detours and modifications along the way. If we find that these changes were productive and useful, and lacking serious contradictions, then perhaps we can all return home feeling self-satisfied and accomplished.

If, on the other hand, our observations tell us that we must make some significant changes or modifications in our struggle in higher education today, and by extension in our struggles in the community, then this paper will have served a most important purpose.

This particular presentation sought to examine those issues and problems which have had and will continue to have an impact on the form and content of our curriculum in Puerto Rican and other ethnic studies. I am hopeful that I have touched upon some issues, problems, and general themes which are familiar to those engaged in the long range struggle to maintain and strengthen ethnic studies in the university.

Notes

1. Queens College Ethnic Studies Council is comprised of six directors each representing an ethnic studies program. These include African Studies, Italian, Jewish, Irish, Greek and Byzantine Studies, and Puerto Rican Studies.

2. Frank Bonilla and Emilio González. "New Knowing, New Practice: Puerto Rican Studies." *Structure of Dependency.* Ford Foundation. Graduate Studies Division, Stamford University, 1973, p. 232.

3. Frank Bonilla, "Colloquium: American Character and Culture in the 1980's: Pluralist Perspectives." Unpublished paper. University of Massachusetts, Boston, September 26, 1980.

4. Fred Hechinger, "Black Studies Come of Age." *New York Times Magazine.* April 13, 1980. p. 48. CF.

5. St. Clair Drake, "What Happened to Black Studies?" *New York University Education Quarterly.* Spring 1979, Volume X, No. 3, pp. 9–16.

6. Lorenzo Middleton. "Black-Studies Professors Say Hard Times will Undermine Struggle for Legitimacy." *The Chronicle of Higher Education.* March 30, 1981.

8

Puerto Rican Studies and Romance Languages: Language and Literature in Puerto Rican Studies

Janice Gordils

The importance of language skills could never be stressed enough. Language is the system of signs, the tools, with which we identify and grasp reality, analyze, and communicate information; it is the system of signs with which we structure thoughts. Furthermore, a language is a cultural code of expression. It conveys the particular cultural experience accumulated by a people throughout their common history, a relatively shared view of the world and of life shaped by that common history, and therefore has no exact equivalent or translation into another language. Language, thus, conditions perception and the identity of the individual, as well as the ability to express and assert one's self and ideas.

As Puerto Ricans living in the United States, we are experiencing a transitional situation in our codes of perception and expression. Whereas since the colonial destruction of the Taino and Carib languages, and the suppression of the language of our African ancestors, our people have expressed their being and reality in Spanish. English is the dominant language of the society we find ourselves in by another turn of colonialism. This historical juncture has been rendering different and varying levels of bilingualism within the country, a bilingualism that cannot be equated to the linguistic transition toward English monolinguism of European immigrants. In contrast to the experience of other nationalities, the retention of the language of Puerto Rico here is conditioned by factors such as the position of the community within the class and racial stratification of this society, and particularly by the circular flow of migration that the politico-economic relationship of Puerto Rico with the U.S. generates. Also, through this circular flow of migration, linguistic changes among the Puerto Ricans living in the United States have repercussions on language usage in Puerto Rico itself.

The current state of this bilingualism is manifest in the varying degrees of competence in English and Spanish of the Hispanic students in Puerto Rican Studies, depending on the social and regional composition of the college, and must be addressed in curricular planning. The Puerto Ricans—and the Latin Americans in general—raised in this country that manage to get to college, as a rule, have not received adequate elementary and high school instruction in Spanish (nor in English, for that matter)—an index of the dismal state of the educational system. The demands that command of other but a prestige dialect of English places on the individual student soon are made evident to the freshmen. Yet, the implications of relegating in formal education the language they first learned to name the world with, are often underestimated. First, the pressures and constraints under which language acquisition takes place affect the development of "acceptable" tools for conceptualization and abstract thinking, and eventually reflect on the special efforts Hispanics have to make in order to adjust to college standards of English, including belated efforts to differentiate both languages in order to minimize syntactical and morphological interferences. Moreover, it is changing our perception of ourselves and of our background and history as a people as the younger generations inherit only a portion of the general culture carried by the family's language—essentially the domestic and affective vocabulary—while being exposed in English to areas and subject matters considered necessary for social and professional mobility (like technical terminology), and to prestigious areas of culture, such as the history of ideas and the fine arts. The process of language fragmentation is thus accompanied by the stratification of the codes of perception and of communication, and, while losing touch with the totality and the "syntax" of the referents of the family's culture and the coherence of the identity (and its worth), of necessity, the vacuum is filled by assimilating in varying degrees, and often in contradictory manner, the values and views on what it is to be Hispanic and Puerto Rican which are imprinted into the English language. The psychological effects of this implicit devaluation of being Puerto Rican or of Hispanic origin are often dramatized if the students, seeking to broaden their command of Spanish, encounter professors who, unfamiliar with the dynamics of languages and insensitive to the specific language needs of the Hispanics raised in this country, downgrade their orally acquired Spanish and regional and class variants as non-Castillian and useless.

(An ahistorical attachment on the part of the professors to Puerto Rican language and culture as inherited from the island is no less harmful.) On the other hand, the English being taught does not fully convey the reality of our people here and now, leading to linguistic and conceptual transculturations (i.e., cultural loans and exchanges) that deserve the most serious attention of our linguists.

Spanish is important to Puerto Rican Studies programs for other academic reasons, namely, that primary sources are mainly available in that language. At least a reading knowledge of Spanish is necessary for both Hispanic and non-Hispanic students in order to pursue more advanced studies in the field. Given the still limited number of sources and textbooks available in English, some knowledge of the language is desirable even to get a fully panoramic view of Puerto Rican culture and avoid the slanted views that could derive from consulting mostly books written by non-Puerto Ricans. On the other hand, Puerto Rican Studies programs cannot put aside every educator's responsibility in the overall formation of the students, and must concurrently attend to the development of skills for analysis and effective expression in English. And this applies to the general population of the courses, and not just to the bilingual or Spanish-speaking students.

The field in which there are less textbooks and sources available in English translation is literature. The importance granted to literature in Puerto Rican Studies curricula is not always as readily or fully understood. Literature—the artistic use of language—is cognitive, and as such it has been understood in our literary tradition. Through its own means and specificity, literature serves to grasp and understand reality and human existence while allowing for subjective expression and aesthetic pleasure. It provides views on personal and individualized experiences and issues in a manner that other fields cannot fully convey; its study refines the individual's ability to communicate in oral and written form.

The character of Latin American literature has to be kept in mind in considering the role of literature courses in Puerto Rican Studies. Literature has played in our societies a more important and broader role than is attributed to it in the Western European tradition. Puerto Rican literature, whether written or oral, has been traditionally produced with an awareness of being a reflection on society, and attempts to act upon it. It is not divided, as often is literature in English, into fiction and non-fiction, and is not primarily produced to entertain, distract, or divert, but rather is aimed at addressing the most urgent issues and problems of our societies, at encompassing the philosophical corpus of our historical formations. Furthermore, when other forms of social and political expression have been curtailed, literature has served as a means to overcome censorship and other limitations, and to affirm our identity, our nationality, and our rights as a people.

The importance of continuing to expose students to the literary productions becomes particularly acute in the face of a tendency within U.S. academia to view Puerto Rico and the Puerto Ricans as a social problem, as another issue reducible to quantitative analysis. While not underestimating the value such studies have, Puerto Rican Studies must continue to stress the interrelationship between all the aspects of a culture and of the life of a people, and that fragmentation for the purpose of analysis must be followed by synthesis or it leads to disintegration, not to knowledge.

The humanities are going through a crisis in the educational system of this country, and in social life in general, as seen, for instance, in the little value attributed to knowing more than one language. The proportions this crisis could reach are reflected in the nationwide cuts in the budgets for studies and endeavors in the humanities. Limited job opportunities in the fields of language and literature—as well as history, philosophy, and the arts—are forcing students into careers where job opportunities are more evident. This is particularly true for the Puerto Ricans who manage to get to college and, unaware of their options, are often routed by counselors and necessity into service oriented careers such as social work. Furthermore, competition within the colleges leads students away from courses not explicitly linked to their career goals. The pressures to address the most immediate needs of the community, to find solutions to every day problems, also lead students—both Puerto Rican and others who take Puerto Rican Studies courses as part of their training to work in Spanish-speaking communities—into instrumental courses and those perceived to be of a more "practical" nature or believed to provide ready-made answers to their concerns.

By maintaining requisites or strongly recommending literature courses, the Puerto Rican Studies programs have been particularly successful in transmitting to the students the fact that, whatever their career goals may be, language skills and literature are not superfluous or could be postponed to periods of leisure as a mere alternative form of entertainment. Indeed, the Puerto Rican community in the U.S. currently needs more lawyers, doctors, and technicians than literature professors, but we need socially responsible and well-informed professionals with broad perspectives on their fields. Puerto Rican Studies cannot, by definition, fall prey to the trend to train students to be efficient machinery, and not thinking and critical human beings in full command over their ideas.

Actually, the task has not been that difficult, since the majority of Hispanic students come to college with some degree of awareness of the psychological and social implications of bilingualism, and of the importance of understanding the cultural and family heritage, as an integral whole, in a hostile environment. Achieving full mastery over Spanish is a challenge to Puerto Rican college students, even when not aware of the job opportunities available to them as bilingual professionals in fields such as media, and as translators and interpreters. Also, our communities have kept alive the tradition of singing, improvising, and writing poetry, and story telling. This develops in the students since early life an appreciation for creative writing that needs to be nurtured in college.

A related problem area is the fact that the current financial and political crisis is further reducing the access of Puerto Ricans and other Hispanics to a college education. As admissions become more competitive, English entry exams are being imposed in a manner that is automatically eliminating many qualifying Hispanic students from higher education.

Budgetary cuts are also having an impact on the availability of resources to develop curricula. Funds for visiting lecturers, visual aids, and for reproduction and acquisition of materials are becoming more scarce and the cost of books is rising. Publishing is becoming more difficult as the cost of paper and printing goes up and the market shrinks, precisely at the point when the research for course preparation and curricular development that has resulted from the last ten years is ready to be published. The need for textbooks, anthologies, and literary criticism is critical. The situation with the needed translations is also critical, and leaves much to be desired, for a bad translation does more harm than helps.

The experience of the past decade has proven that the strong language and literature policies of Puerto Rican Studies programs have been correct. Enriched by this experience, and considering the problems faced by the humanities in general, what shall we include in the agenda for the 1980s? What follows are some suggestions submitted for discussion:

1. We must continue to work toward an increased awareness on the part of the students—and of the community in general—of the importance of language skills in their overall formation, and why the access to education in Spanish has been such a heated issue in the U.S. as well as in Puerto Rico. Both goals are intertwined in courses as the traditional "Language in Puerto Rico," now enriched by new materials and data on the Spanish spoken in the U.S. But also this needs to be addressed for the perspective of other disciplines, such

as law, as professor and lawyer Manuel del Valle has been doing for several years at Yale, Princeton, and Fordham; or in a sociology course designed by Prof. María Torres del Valle, Fordham University, entitled "Language Loyalty and the Puerto Rican Community."

2. Through counseling, students should be better informed of careers where a native command of Spanish is an asset. Media has been mentioned; linguistics is another, as there are very few linguists specialized in Spanish in this country.

3. The changing language dominance of the students must be under constant scrutiny in order to show the adequacy of the courses and avoid a possible gap between the professors' plans and expectations and the concrete needs of the incoming students.

4. The importance of literature must be self-evident in the design of the courses, which must be meaningful, accessible, and up to date. Literature courses need not be historical accounts of dead letters; they must be meaningful today or become mere scholastic exercises. The traditional chronological surveys of major works and authors needs revision, or at least to be complemented. A more critical and analytical approach to our literature and its history is often better served by grouping works and authors around trends, issues, and schools of thought rather than focusing on the individual authors. And, these courses should have as one of their main objectives to develop analytical and critical reading skills.

5. Literature courses should continue to incorporate comparative perspectives. Puerto Rican literature is part of Latin American literature and particularly of Caribbean literature, a fact that should not be taken for granted. It is illuminating to students to see this parentage inherent in the works themselves by comparing stylistic, thematic, and ideological trends.

6. At his point in time the literature produced about the Puerto Rican experience in the U.S. is significant. This needs to be better and more critically integrated into the curriculum, not just as a separate course on what has been termed "Neorican" literature, but as part of a literary heritage. The comparative approach is also appropriate here; we need to become more knowledgeable of Chicano literary production, as well as of the points of coincidence and differences with U.S. and Afro-American literature. An example of the comparative approach from Fordham's curriculum is a thematic course I taught which encompasses the migratory experience in Puerto Rican literature since the first half of the nineteenth century as viewed from inside and outside the Island, and also makes references to comparable experiences as that of the West Indians living in London and in Paris.

7. Oral and popular literature should play a more important role in the curriculum; the study of the dominant literature simply does not suffice.

8. Courses should make the widest use possible of the resources available outside the colleges, and at the same time contribute to the students' awareness of the cultural and artistic activities available to the community. An area where this is particularly desirable is the theater arts.

9. Students should be exposed to literary writing in other courses, not just in the straight literature courses. Essays by Puerto Rican thinkers should be included in history and sociology reading lists in a more systematic way, contributing to the students' exposure to primary sources.

10. Language and literature courses should make more space for active and productive student participation. Among other possible student projects, consider: (a) engaging students in the collection of oral literature and testimonies among the members of their families, in their neighborhoods, and in their communities and work centers; (b) students could also help compile the literary production dispersed in Spanish newspapers published in this country since the beginning of the last century, the quality of which puts to shame many current journalistic publications; (c) more and better translators are needed, and students could develop translation skills as part of their course work and at the same time contribute much needed translations.

11. On the professors' side, we need to produce more literary criticism, must continue developing more critical approaches to our literary heritage. An example of the kind of works needed is Juan Flores' ideological analysis of Pedreira's *Insularismo*.

12. But, of course, these works must be published in order to be of use to the community as a whole, and not just to one program. Within each Puerto Rican Studies program much literary criticism has developed side by side with course preparations; very little has been published. A collective effort might be necessary in order to open up access to publishing facilities with wide distribution, and to do away with stereotypical views on Puerto Rican literature.

13. There is also a need to share more the ongoing research. Steps in this direction could be: a. to regularly schedule seminars involving language and literature professors and researchers in Puerto Rican Studies; b. to develop alternative forms to formal publication of finished works. Works in progress could be exchanged in the form of mimeographed pamphlets with a view to publication after receiving the critique of colleagues in the field, much in the manner the Center for Puerto Rican Studies has been doing.

14. We must continue our efforts to overcome the tendency within some colleges to isolate Puerto Rican Studies from the mainstream of academic life. Literature courses in Puerto Rican Studies should *also* be part of the Spanish major, for instance. The reasons for establishing Puerto Rican Studies a decade ago are still the reasons for the existence of the programs, and marginalization contradicts them.

15. One problem area mentioned that has not been addressed in this proposition for a plan of action is the reduced access of our community to higher education. This touches on language and literature to the degree that class-biased entry exams in English are screening out qualifying Hispanic students, but the problem is political, and as such it must be addressed.

A neologism has been gaining currency in the past few years when contending that, as a community, the Puerto Ricans living in the U.S. are risking a situation of nilinguism, that is, of losing the full range of expression in Spanish while not having access to an education that would provide full proficiency in standard English. This would amount to deculturation, as opposed to acculturation, that is, to being left with a limited cultural range, with reduced tools to express one's perception of reality and to effect changes. Although sociolinguistic studies disprove the claims of nilinguism or alinguism,[1] the fact remains that working class Hispanic students entering college often develop an amount of insecurity in their language proficiency, whether justified or not. And a person insecure of his or her tools of expression is less likely to challenge the way he or she is characterized by others, less likely to effectively stand up for his or her ideas, and more susceptible to submitting to the views and opinions advanced by others.

The claims of nilinguism are considered more or less relevant depending on the weight attributed to the impact language changes among the Puerto Ricans in the United States have in Puerto Rico through the return and circular migration, and are rooted in a historic fear for the survival of the Puerto Rican people. Indeed, this is not the first time that the people of Puerto Rico are challenged with the pressures to acculturate through language. When Spain colonized Puerto Rico, the imposition of Spanish was a clearly stated policy, as expressed in the prologue to the first grammar of a Western European language, Nebrija's: "language is the instrument of empires," an idea Machiavelli incorporated into his *Prince*. Under this policy, the aboriginal Taino and Carib population lost their language and forcefully had to accept the colonizers' view of life and of themselves, disappearing as a people in fifty years. The experience was repeated with the African slaves, who inherited a language that portrayed them as inferior to the masters and thus deserving slavery and discrimination. The United States assumed a similar policy when the island was occupied in 1898 and "the work of remaking Puerto Rico into a possession of the U.S. commenced," wrote Governor Theodore Roosevelt, with a "resolute attempt to stamp out local customs and culture and to substitute English for Spanish."[2]

The name of the original inhabitants of Puerto Rico, five centuries after their extinction, is still associated with the term "docile," as Columbus called them, and it has taken several centuries for the word "negrito" (the diminutive of Negro) to become a colorless term of endearment. Now "Puerto Rican" has to be rid of the connotations it has acquired in this society, so that (to use an example dear to my colleague Julio Marzán) it is not shocking to read in the press "Puerto Rican scientist," for the translation of "puertorriqueño" to express what we are instead of what we a supposedly lacking (non-white, non-English-speaking, etc.)

Although this task is not linguistic, for language is but a reflection of other spheres of social life; Puerto Rican Studies has a role to play in developing the students literate awareness, so that their choice of words and syntax—in English and in Spanish—expresses an enriched choice of ways among available options. Thus in assuming the *lingua franca* of this society as also our language we are broadening our literary and cultural range, not uncritically submitting to the values and ready-made views on what to be Puerto Rican and of Hispanic origin that have been embedded in English or relinquishing our rights as members of a pluralistic society, nor the right to determine our destiny as a people.

Notes

1. *Vide, The Language Policy Task Force Working Papers.* The Centro de Estudios Puertorriqueños.

2. Cited in *Colonial Policies of the United States.* New York: Doubleday, Doran & Co., 1937.

9

Puerto Rican Studies
and Political Economy

Pedro Cabán

This paper provides an overview for the organization of a course on the political economy of Puerto Rico. Despite the prevalence of alternative notions of what constitutes a political economy perspective, there is sufficient consensus among numerous practitioners in the discipline on the minimal essential components of such an approach.

The course as presently organized employs a political economy approach which focuses on the social class structure and distinguishes among classes in terms of their relationship to the instruments of production. A second theme stresses that the state apparatus lacks the autonomy to abrogate the structural requirements of a capitalist economy; these requirements include the use of wage labor to realize surplus value, the protection of private appropriation of collectively realized surplus, and the preservation of a stable environment for capital accumulation.

By virtue of its status as a colonial possession, Puerto Rico has evolved a social class structure which responds to the material bases determined by the exigencies of capitalist production in the metropolitan centers. Although this pattern of insertion into the global economy is not unique, it does require a mode of analysis which examines the specifically colonial features of capitalist development in Puerto Rico. Elements in this analysis include the interconnections between the metropolitan state apparatus with its surrogate administrative structure in the colony; changes in colonial administrative structure which both paralleled and facilitated the progressive evolution of distinct types of capitalist development; and responses by the metropolitan colonial state nexus to political contradictions which persistently emerge in Puerto Rico.

These concepts provide a framework for a course on the political economy of Puerto Rico. But a curriculum, or for that matter simply a course, should have a common theme which links seemingly disparate developments in the nation's complex historical evolution.

It appears that a useful theme is the structure of capital accumulation during specific historical conjunctures. The operating assumption is that the structure of capital accumulation have been shaped by the requirements of capitalist expansion or contraction in the metropole. The accumulation can be measured in terms of the ownership of the means of production, the organization of the productive forces, investment rates, sectoral allocation of productive inputs, application of technology consistent with profit maximization, and public expenditures on infrastructure development and maintenance. We can generally identity three historical periods in which there was a significant restructuring of the process in which socially produced surplus was privately appropriated. The curriculum is thus divided into three historical periods, and within each of these periods the structure of capital accumulation, and how it relates to other economic, political and social changes will be analyzed. The historical periods which roughly correspond to alterations in the process and structure of accumulation are:

The period of European economic and political domination of Puerto Rico (This period extends roughly from the colonization in the late 1490s until the American invasion of 1898.)

This initial section examines the precapitalist modes of production and social organizations established by the indigenous populations of Puerto Rico. After this discussion, the course examines the violent displacement of the indigenous populations by the Spanish, and the implantation of new modes of production. These modes evolved from slave labor to debt peonage and precapitalist wage labor corresponding to changes in the form of Puerto Rico's insertion in the international economy.

Following the work of CEREP (Spanish acronym for the Study of the Puerto Rican Reality a private research agency based in San Juan) and the Centro de Estudios Puertorriqueños the section examines the increasing political conflict between the *criollo* agro-exporting sector made up of native Puerto Rican owners and the peninsular-dominated commercial and export sectors controlled by Spanish nationals. Emphasis is be placed on how the demands of capitalist expansion in Europe and on Spain's undeveloped economy affected the formation of indigenous capitalist forces. This analysis leads to a discussion of the patterns of social class formation and organization or political forces through the late 1890s.

The period of economic domination from 1898 through 1948

The major themes in this section are the implantation of a political-administrative structure which operated to facilitate North American penetration and control of the productive resources of Puerto Rico, and the enforced conversion of the insular economy into an intensive monocrop export-oriented productive system. This section also analyzes the organization of working class and the formation of a rural proletariat. It was during this period that nationalistic forces challenging North American imperialism emerged. At the same time reform-minded political leaders of an emasculated Puerto Rican bourgeoisie began to agitate for reforms. Finally, the second part examines changes in the institutional arrangements through which the United States exercised control over political and economic forces on the island.

The period of industrialization and the creation of a welfare state: from 1948 to the present

This section assesses the evolution of the contemporary dependent capitalist economics of Puerto Rico. Themes which will be examined include the aborted attempts by reform-minded state managers to develop a pattern of capital accumulation consistent with changes in Puerto Rico's position in the international economy. These attempts included state capitalist enterprises in light manufacturing and infra-structure, state appropriation of collectively realized surplus, and acquisition of productive lands for redistribution to direct producers. This section also discusses the specific policies implemented by the metropolitan colonial nexus to fashion a system of production and accumulation which optimized the rate of return on foreign investments. The discussion also focuses on the strategies employed to contain the socially disruptive aspects of this type of development model, which included enforced emigration of surplus labor, labor absorption through the expansion of public sector employment. Finally, the section concludes with a brief discussion of the international division of labor and the consequences that this latest unfolding of capitalist development has generated for Puerto Rico.

Although the available English language material on the theoretical subjects addressed in the course is abundant, there is very little written specifically about Puerto Rico. However some recent works of solid theoretical quality, and which reinterpret aspects of Puerto Rico's political economy are available, and would be assigned for the course. I will note the Centro de Estudios Puertorriqueños' *Labor Migration Under Capitalism*; José J. Villamil's *Transnational Capitalism and National Development*; James Petras' equally brief statement in

Critical Perspectives on Imperialism, some of the essays, principally those of Quintero Rivera, which appear in Adalberto López' recent work, *The Puerto Ricans,* as important sources. The works of Laird Bergad, Fernando Picó, and John Wessman on the economic history of agrarian Puerto Rico also deserve mention. Various studies of CEREP, although written in Spanish would be translated for class adoption. The writings of Bernado Vega and Jesus Colon, among others, provide significant resource material and interpretive texts that are relevant for the course.

In short, although there is not a basic text, sufficient material exists which the enterprising and dedicated instructor could utilize for the course.

I envision a variety of problems engendered in such a course. The organization and content of the course is controversial for it appears to overlook the emergence of nationalist forces in the Puerto Rican reality. The question of institutional reaction to this pedagogical approach which seeks to advance an ongoing critical theoretical debate is a matter that both the instructor and the academic unit must confront. Finally, another concern is how the instructor imaginatively links the abstract conceptual elements of the course with the empirical referents in order to expand students' understanding of the interplay of political and economic forces in Puerto Rico's development.

It would appear to me that this course should not be artificially separated from other courses in the Puerto Rican Studies curriculum. Rather a series of interrelated courses which examine specific developmental episodes should be designed. There is a need to transcend the differentiated and compartmentalized concerns of the social science disciplines, and to search for the most productive cross-fertilization of these disciplines. I will argue that the fabric which links courses in a Puerto Rican Studies curriculum should be an approach which examines the evolution of Puerto Rican society in both the metropole and the colony from a historical structuralistic perspective. I will also cautiously advance the suggestions that a tentative effort should be made by us to discuss more fully the anticipated organizational features and economic structures of an autonomous post colonial society.

Finally, I would like to make a plea for the establishment of a network of interested folks which could meet on a regular basis to discuss their research, writings, or ideas on various aspects of the Puerto Rican reality in accordance with a structural-historical analytical perspective. There is a need for such a system of interaction; this forum could serve to initiate a dialogue along these other mutually acceptable lines.

I entertain no illusions that curriculum recommendations will result in an acceptance of a more critical perspective that interprets the evolution of Puerto Rican reality, not as isolated and ideosyncratic historical episode, but as a reflection of world capitalist development. This analytical perspective, with its emphasis on state structures, social class conflict, and transnational capitalism, is alien to some and smacks of unbridled radicalism to others. However, I could hope that, as a minimum, students would question the salience of ethnic chauvinism as a principle factor explaining the persistent attempts at national exploitation and subjugation.

10
Puerto Rican Studies and Anthropology: We Are a Caribbean People

Rafael L. Ramírez

The discussion of the relationship between anthropology and Puerto Rican Studies must consider three major questions. What is anthropology? What type of anthropology will be introduced in the curriculum? How the adoption of an anthropological approach could modify the theory and practice of Puerto Rican Studies? Although anthropology is a holistic discipline it is divided in four major fields: biological anthropology; linguistics; archeology; and sociocultural anthropology. Each field is subsequently divided in several areas of specialization. At present the discipline is also characterized by a diversity of theoretical approaches and several schools of anthropological thought. The relationship between the different fields and the uniqueness of anthropology as a social sciences discipline is achieved through the integration of the biocultural approach, the comparative method, and the historical dimension. A definition of anthropology that may guide our discussion is: "The analysis of the interaction of human beings with their environment, as well as the study of social institutions and social processes with a comparative and historical approach."

The purpose of this section is to discuss how to operationalize the adoption of an anthropological approach in the curriculum of Puerto Rican Studies. One or several courses in anthropology is not part of our proposal. What we suggest is the incorporation of the theoretical and methodological approaches of anthropology, as previously defined, in existing courses, or the development of new courses in which the three major approaches of anthropology are included.

First: the biocultural approach analyzes the interaction between biological and sociocultural factors in human populations. Among its topics are included the process of biological adaptation, the evolution of human capacity for culture, Mendelian inheritance, and population genetics. This type of analysis will provide a comprehension of the biological diversity of Puerto Ricans (both geno- and phenotypical), the nature of gene flow, and the social factors which interact with gene flow. It will also make a significant contribution to clarify how the concept of race is used, its lack of precision as a scientific instrument to understand human variability, the interaction between nature and nurture, the essence of racism, and the meaning of ethnicity. This approach also contributes to the integration of the biological and the social sciences.

Second: the comparative approach provides an understanding of elements common to all human societies, and the sociocultural strategies developed by different societies to face the challenges posed by the environment, social reproduction, the maintenance of an orderly social life, and the transmission of values and belief systems. The proposal is to adopt a method of controlled comparison in which Puerto Rican society and the Puerto Rican experience is analyzed within the Caribbean context. *Somos un pueblo caribeño.* We share a common history with other Caribbean societies which precedes Western conquest and colonization. We also share a colonial heritage, slavery, the problems of underdevelopment and dependency, as well as cultural institutions. The isolation of Caribbean societies from one another is a consequence of Western imperialism and part of the relationship between the colony and the metropolis. Puerto Rican Studies should not contribute to maintain the isolation imposed upon us by colonial powers and colonized politicians. Another area in which the comparative approach could be included is in the analysis of migration. Puerto Rican migration is not unique. It is part of the movement of labor and capital within the Caribbean region (including Central America), and to the United States, Canada, France, and England. An adequate understanding of migratory movements of Puerto Ricans will not be provided to students if our migration is not compared to the phenomenon of migration within and from the Caribbean region.

Third: it is not necessary to explain and justify the historical dimension. However, our history did not start with Cristobal Colón (Columbus); the history of Puerto Rico and the Caribbean should be traced to the first movements of human populations from the Orinoco region to the Antilles. Ethnolinguistics, archeology, and ethnohistory of the Caribbean region should be included in the curriculum. Otherwise the students will have a parochial view and a limited comprehension of Puerto Rico and the development of its social institutions.

Fourth: the preservation and enrichment of the Spanish language must have a top priority in a program of Puerto Rican Studies. Ideally, the students should develop basic skills in the three major languages of the Caribbean: French, Spanish, and English.

Fifth: the progressive urbanization of Puerto Rico and the large concentration of Puerto Rican migrants in urban areas of the United States mean that, from an anthropological perspective, the curriculum has to offer courses in urban studies relevant to the Puerto Rican experience.

It is impossible to provide a detailed bibliography at this point. The selective bibliography consists of major sources which should be read by every student in the Puerto Rican Studies program.

Bastide, Roger. *African Civilizations in the New World*. New York: Harper & Row, 1971.

Centro de Estudios Puertorriqueños. History Task Force. *Labor Migration Under Capitalism. The Puerto Rican Experience*. New York: Monthly Review Press, 1979.

Duncan, Ronald J., editor. *The Anthropology of the People of Puerto Rico*. San Germán: Interamerican University Press, 1978.

Galeano, Eduardo. *Las Venas Abiertas de América Latina*. México: Siglo XXI, 1971.

Guerra, Ramiro. *Sugar and Society in the Caribbean*. New Haven: Yale University Press, 1964.

Horowitz, Michael M. *Peoples and Cultures of the Caribbean*. New York: The Natural History Press, 1971.

Lewis, Gordon K. *Puerto Rico: Freedom and Power in the Caribbean*. New York: Monthly Review Press, 1963.

———. *The Growth of the Modern West Indies*. New York: Monthly Review Press, 1968.

Leyburn, James G. *The Haitian People*. New Haven: Yale University Press, 1966.

López-Baralt, Mercedes. *El Mito Taíno: Raíz y Proyecciones en la Amazonia Continental*. Río Piedras: Huracán, 1976.

Ortiz, Fernando. *Contrapunteo Cubano del Azúcar y el Tabaco*. Barcelona: Arial, 1973.

Steward, Julian H. *The People of Puerto Rico*. Urbana: University of Illinois Press, 1956.

Sued Badillo, Jalil. *Los Caribes: Realidad o Fábula*. Río Piedras: Editorial Antillana, 1978.

Williams, Eric. *Capitalism and Slavery*. London: Andre Deutsch, 1964.

_____. *From Columbus to Castro: The History of the Caribbean 1492-1969*. New York: Harper & Row, 1970.

The first problem is that in order to incorporate the biocultural approach to the curriculum of Puerto Rican Studies some prerequisites must be satisfied. One, the students need a background in elementary biology and introductory physical anthropology. Two, it may be necessary to have an anthropologist (with some training in physical anthropology) on the staff of the Puerto Rican Studies programs. Otherwise arrangements can be made with the Department of Anthropology in the different institutions. Another aspect of the problem is the scarcity of published materials on the population genetics of Puerto Ricans. There is only one human geneticist in Puerto Rico; there are no physical anthropologists. Research on human and population genetics from an anthropological perspective is practically non-existent. The second problem is the comparative approach. How can the required background on Caribbean social institutions can be offered without duplicating the offerings of the Caribbean Studies programs? Is it possible to establish collaboration with the latter? Do we need a separate entity called Puerto Rican Studies? Should we include the analysis of Puerto Rican society within the large framework of Caribbean Studies? In sum, what is the relationship between Puerto Rican and Caribbean Studies? The third problem has to do with the language policy. Do we all agree that mastering of the Spanish language should be required in a Puerto Rican Studies program? Is there enough institutional support for such a policy?

The discipline of anthropology can make significant contributions to the curriculum. We need highly trained anthropologists, and the collaboration of other anthropologists interested in Puerto Rico and the Caribbean. A long-range goal should be to encourage Puerto Rican students to enroll in Ph.D. programs in anthropology. However, institutional support for this discipline is dwindling. There is also a relative scarcity of academic positions. As a result, admission to graduate programs is limited and highly competitive. Efforts should be made to provide students with adequate advice, and to search for economic support (fellowships, grants) to guarantee their opportunities to become professional anthropologists. With respect to Puerto Rican Studies in general, alternatives to the present institutional organization could be explored. One alternative is to promote more joint appointments with other academic departments. Another, to discuss the possibility of establishing a Puerto Rican College of high-academic standards, where our students could be trained in the arts and sciences, and at the same time be exposed to an educational experience which would allow them to develop their identity, their consciousness, and an awarness of their responsibilities to the Puerto Rican community.

I propose that a committee of Puerto Rican anthropologists be formed to develop the guidelines for the incorporation of anthropology in the curriculum of Puerto Rican Studies.

11
Puerto Rican Studies and Sociology

Juan E. Hernández-Cruz

This paper provides an overview for the organization of a course on Sociology and Puerto Rican Studies. The framework for such a course should be directed to a systematic study of intergroup relations, and especially the dominant-minority form, characteristic of the United States-Puerto Rico relationship.

The treatment of dominant-minority relations as a theme of contemporary sociology can be focused upon colonialism and migration, the two types of situations in which the groups meet. Colonialism is an invasion that allows the incoming group to impose its values on the colonized. Migration, on the other hand, generally places the incoming group into a disadvantageous situation regarding society's values.

Of these two types of situations the first, colonialism, has been neglected by most traditional sociologists. Instead, the Malthusian[1] perspective and the assimilation process dominate the analysis of the Puerto Rican experience.

Disregarding the impact of colonialism, mainland sociologists assume that Puerto Ricans are in the United States because they do not "fit" on the Island. In such a view, migration is seen as economically necessary; sociologists argue that Puerto Rican migration to the United States has been beneficial to both countries and to the migrants themselves.[2]

For sociologists within this perspective, the main cause of Puerto Rican migration is the disparity between population growth and development in the sending country. However, in their analysis, the conditions of underdevelopment are not tied to a particular mode of production which may create and expand the gap between population and employment opportunities. For most of them, the economic growth of a country is equated to per-capita income, and migration is significant because it has the effect of reducing unemployment figures.

Essentially, the assimilation approach stresses the "selective characteristic" and "motivations for the move" of the migrants within a comparative approach with the ones remaining at home and the population of the host society. Thus, the causes of emigration are seen in terms of "push and pull" factors affecting the motivations of migrants. In this view, the Puerto Ricans are seen as "newcomers" in the process of incorporation of minorities into the United States' society, properly motivated toward assimilation.[3] Assumptions are also made of the "superiority" of the migrants,[4] and that "integration" and "assimilation" will likely take place within a generation or two.[5]

Problems pertaining to Puerto Rican culture, social stratification, and family structures are, therefore, understood, discussed, and assessed by most sociologists from the point of view that mirrors the values of the dominant society. A case in point is the typical sociological assessment of the Puerto Rican family. Intimate relationships with the kinship system of the extended family are of high value and a source of pride and security to Puerto Ricans, but many sociologists in the United States define the extended family as "pathological." They suggest that these values interfere with the decision-making process and with the mobility of the nuclear unit in an impersonal industrial society. Likewise, consensual unions, a common cultural practice among the Puerto Ricans, have also been labeled negatively by the same sociologists, because such nonformalized conjugal unions are supposedly "non-stable."

A new theoretical perspective has emerged as a result of the awareness of scholars and students of the 1960s who argued that the immigrant analogy widely used to study European minorities in the United States was not applicable to the Blacks, Chicanos, or Puerto Ricans.[6]

Puerto Rican scholars influenced by this perspective turned to the material conditions of Puerto Rico for an explanation of migration. They focused upon the prevailing mode of production, economic underdevelopment, and colonialism; they linked Puerto Rican migration to the United States with unemployment and overpopulation on the Island, reassessed return migration as a circulatory movement of workers, searching for employment among companies searching for profits.

The studies under this new perspective use two different interpretations and are divided as follows: one, those that overtly utilized a Marxist interpretation in the analysis of Puerto Rican migration or "circulation of workers"[7]; two, those that question migration trends and their effect upon the Island's society and/or the North American scholar's interpretation of the Puerto Rican migration experience, without directly acknowledging a Marxist perspective. A major concern of this second group is the role assumed by the Puerto Rican migration of depressing wage levels and increasing the ranks of the industrial reserve army in cities like New York at an historical moment when the material conditions offered no one to queue up after the Puerto Ricans.[8]

For the proponents of this emerging theoretical framework, the subsequent absorption of the Puerto Rican economy into that of the United States, and the lack of autonomy and decision-making control,[9] and the capitaist mode of production on the Island[10] are the main reasons for the perception of overpopulation on the island. Furthermore, these scholars reconceptualize overpopulation as a "relative surplus population" or an "industrial reserve army" produced by the capitalist mode of production. Thus, the majority of the working class in Puerto Rico and of the Puerto Ricans in the United States occupy virtually the same economic and social function for the capitalist economy.[11]

For these scholars, there could be no universal law of population as stated by Malthus; existing "overpopulation" is not to be found in biological proclivities, but in the prevailing capitalist mode of production. Population, they suggest, has a Marxist meaning: the social classes contained in a specific mode of production and the interrelationships among them. Whether by colonialism or by migration, the capitalist mode of production creates its own relative surplus population or the army of unemployed, independently of the actual rate of population increase.

Overpopulation occurs when capital accumulation, variable capital, and source of demand for work do not keep pace with the increase of working population. This conditions creates the material conditions for the exodus of the working class, who migrate with the expectation of obtaining the employment not found at home. In this respect, Marx observed, in a series of articles about the Irish question:

> . . . with modern compulsory emigration the case stands quite opposite. Here it is not the want of productive power which creates a surplus population; it is the increase of productive power which demands a dimunition of population, and drives away the surplus by famine and emigration. It is not the population that presses on productive power; it is productive power that presses on population.[12]

Therefore, the economic structures of colonialism are the historical causes of emigration, and the point of departure for sociological analysis of Puerto Rican migration should be its colonial relationships. Underdevelopment and overpopulation ought to be seen as the products of the historical, economic, social, and political relations with the dominant power, be it Spain or the United States.

Studies concerned with the experience of Puerto Ricans in the United States and interpretative documents stressing the traditional view of Malthusianism and assimilation are: Lawrence Chenault, _The Puerto Rican Migration in New York City_ (New York: Russell and Russell 1938); C. W. Mills, Clarence Senior, and Rose Goldsen, _The Puerto Rican Journey_ (New York: Harper, 1950); Nathan Glazer, and Daniel Moynihan, _Beyond the Melting Pot_ (Cambridge, Mass.: M.I.T. and Harvard University Press, 1963); Joseph Fitzpatrick, _Puerto Rican Americans: The Meaning of Migration to the Mainland._ (Englewood Cliffs, New Jersey: Prentice Hall, 1971); Clarence Senior, _Puerto Rican Migration._ (Río Piedras: Social Science Research Center, University of Puerto Rico, 1947); Clarence Senior and Donald O. Watkings, "Toward a Balance Sheet of Puerto Rican Migration," _United States-Puerto Rican Commission on the Status of Puerto Rico, August, 1966; International Migration Review_ II, no. 2, (1968).

The works following the newest perspective are: Centro de Estudios Puertorriqueños, _Taller de Migración: Conferencia de Historiografía: Abril, 1974_ (bilingual edition) (New York: Research Foundation of the City University of New York, 1975); Manuel Maldonado Denis, _Puerto Rico y Estados Unidos: Emigración v Colonialismo._ (México: Siglo XXI Editores S. A.: 1976). Also, in English: _The Emigration Dialectic: Puerto Rico and the U.S.A._ (New York: International Publishers, 1980); History Task Force, Centro, _Labor Migration Under Capitalism: The Puerto Rican Experience_ (New York: Monthly Review Press, 1979); José L. Vásquez Calzada, "La Emigración Puertorriqueña: ¿Solución o Problema?" Also, "Demographic Aspects of Migration," _Labor Migration Under Capitalism_, 223-36; Adalberto López and James Patras, _Puerto Rico and the Puerto Ricans: Studies in History and Society_ (New York: Schenckman Publishing Co., 1974); Luis Nieves Falcón, _El Emigrante Puertorriqueño_ (Río Piedras: Editorial Edil, 1976); Clara Rodríguez, "A Cost Benefit Analysis of Subjective Factors Affecting Assimilation: Puerto Ricans," _Ethnicity_, 2:66–80 (1975); also, "Economic Factors Affecting Puerto Ricans in New York," _Labor Migration Under Capitalism_, 197-221. The first study to highlight the concept of circular migration is still relevant: José Hernández, _Return Migration to Puerto Rico_ (Berkeley: University of California Press, 1967).

More recent books include Virginia Sanchez Korrol, *From Colonia to Community: The History of Puerto Ricans in New York City, 1917–1948* (Westport, Ct.: Greenwood Press, 1983), in which the experiences of pioneer migrants in New York settlements are reassessed. Together with survey articles such as the one by Antonio M. Stevens-Arroyo and Ana María Díaz in *the Minority Report*, (New York: Holt, Rinehart and Winston, 2nd edition 1982), and Clara Rodriguez, Virginia Sanchez Korrol, and Oscar Alers, eds., *The Puerto Rican Struggles: Essays in Survival* (Maplewood, New Jersey: Waterfront Press, 1984), there is a slowly growing literature of significant resource materials and interpretative texts that are relevant for a comparative approach on the topic. More research and publications are needed in the areas of social stratification, family, and the community.

A major pedagogical problem in teaching any sociological course in Puerto Ricans is the role of critical thinking. Most students are not used to questioning the premises of textbook authors or searching for bias. The interdisciplinary character of this new curriculum introduces another obstacle, placing great demands on faculty, who must be aware of the continuous theoretical and methodological debate that takes place in the social sciences. Mechanisms should be developed to enable an ongoing study, probably by alternating teaching and research. Finally, student expectations, coupled with the emotional and personal nature of the subject matter, enlarge the role of teacher into that of mentor.

Since social research among racial and ethnic minorities presents unique theoretical and methodological challenges requiring the use of special methodological procedures and techniques, an institutional commitment to research must be negotiated with university administration. We need to develop highly trained sociologists interested in Puerto Rican and Caribbean realities. Research among racial and ethnic minorities is in its initial stages, and scholars must be close enough to the people in order to be sensitive to their problems. This would seem the best mode of shaping new theories and methodologies for assessing and understanding contemporary experiences.

Many higher education institutions would have reservations about sponsoring this type of research. Theirs is a common bias against researchers who are themselves minority group members. Moreover in situations often fear that the minority peoples will be studied from an advocacy position. Mindful of these factors, I recommend the widening of a network of interested scholars and community leaders which could meet to discuss strategies to deal with the problems of funded research and how to influence university policies.

In conclusion, I am optimistic that these new theoretical and methodological perspectives will eventually have to be recognized for their logical consequences and for the rigor employed in the development. I am also optimistic about the contributions Puerto Rican Studies are making to the stock of learning in the various fields, from literature to political science and from the arts to sociology. In my view, such should be our goals in a future agenda of renaissance: keeping research responsive to teaching needs, the further development of faculty, and publishing these findings in accurate and accessible fashion.

Notes

1. Malthus' theory rested upon the supposition that man's capacity to increase his means of subsistence was much less than his capacity to multiply. He asserted that man could increase his subsistence only in arithmetical progression, while his numbers tended to increase in geometrical progression. The history of mankind demonstrated, Malthus said, that population always tended toward the limit set by subsistence and was contained within that limit by the operation of positive and preventive checks. The checks—want, famine, pestilence, and premature mortality—were all resolvable into terms of "misery" and "vice." Emigration was also viewed by him as a temporary palliative to population pressure. See, Thomas Robert Malthus, *An Essay on the Principle of Population* (London, n. p., 1803).

2. Lawrence Chenault, *The Puerto Rican Migration in New York City* (New York: Russell and Russell, 1938); C. Wright Mills, Clarence Senior, and Rose Goldsen, *The Puerto Rican Journey* (New York: Harper, 1950); Nathan Glazer and Daniel P. Moynihan, *Beyond the Melting Pot* (Cambridge, Mass: MIT Press, 1963); Joseph P. Fitzpatrick, S. J., *Puerto Rican Americans; The Meaning of Migration to the Mainland* (Englewood Cliffs: Prentice-Hall, 1971).

3. Glazer and Moynihan, p. 62; Fitzpatrick, p. 45.

4. Clarence Senior, *Puerto Rican Migration* (Río Piedras: Social Science Research Center, 1947).

5. Milton A. Gordon, *Assimilation in American Life* (New York: Oxford University Press, 1964); John J. Macisco, "Assimilation of Puerto Ricans on the Mainland: A Sociodemographic Approach," *International Migration Review* 2 (Spring 1968).

6. Blauner suggested that America was holding its minorities within its boundaries in a quasi-colonial status. See, Robert Blauner, "Black Culture: Myth or Reality?" in Norman E. Whitten, Jr. and John F. Szwed, eds., *Afro-American Anthropology* (New York: The Free Press, 1970), pp. 347–66.

7. Centro de Estudios Puertorriqueños, *Labor Migration Under Capitalism: The Puerto Rican Experience* (New York: Monthly Review Press, 1979); Manuel Maldonado Denis, *The Emigration Dialectic: Puerto Rico and the U.S.A.* (New York: International Publishers, 1980).

8. Clara Rodriquez, in *Labor Migration*, p. 198.

9. Adalberto Lopez and James Petras, *Puerto Rico and the Puerto Ricans: Studies in History and Society* (New York: Schenkman, 1974).

10. Maldonado-Denis, *The Emigration Dialectic;* Centro, Labor Migration.

11. Centro, *Ibid.,* p. 49.

12. Karl Marx and Fredrich Engels, *Ireland and the Irish Question* (Moscow: Progress Publishers, 1971), p. 57.

12
Puerto Rican Studies and Social Service Careers

Julio Morales

In the material I received from the organizers of this anthology I was instructed to keep my introduction short "since the contextualization of the conference will supply for the formalities of presentation." The material also said the seminal papers would "be subjected to considerable scrutiny, and in all honesty, only those persons who combine gifts of both scholarship and humility can be expected to rise to this challenge." After reading those statements, I was petrified and certain that I had made an error in having accepted the task which I had undertaken since I see myself as more of an organizer and doer than a scholar, have always had difficulty being humble, and was looking forward to a lengthy introduction in whch I nostalgically and somewhat in shock reminisced about my four years at Brooklyn College as one of the two initial faculty members charged with developing a Puerto Rican Studies Institute and later a Puerto Rican Studies Department.

In tackling the theme of Puerto Rican Studies Curriculum and Social Service Careers I must commence by attempting to define some terms and raising some questions.

In the first place Puerto Rican Studies sounds very specific and yet I would plead for a broad interpretation of that phrase to include, one, knowledge and appreciation of Puerto Rican history, culture and language; two, an understanding of the forces leading to our oppression as a people. This understanding should move us to both anger and a commitment to a protractive struggle aimed at ending that oppression, and joining forces with other oppressed groups in building for a more humane society for all people; and three, expertise in a specific arena of organized academic and/or non-academic activity with some flexible but tangible parameters (such as education, economics, research, social work, language, politics, art, etc.), which would enable us to put into practice our knowledge and appreciation of our history and culture, our understanding of oppression, and our specific dedication and commitment to that group of people who form the Puerto Rican nation as well as to other disenfranchised peoples. This definition is especially important when we start discussing Puerto Rican Studies Curriculum and Social Service Careers.

Secondly, Social Service Careers is too broad a category. It not only includes all of the traditional social work methods of casework, group work, community organization, social planning and administration, but usually counseling, therapy, public assistance determination, job training, housing and health advocacy, urban planning, service provision, etc. These careers involve training ranging from educational programs that require no formal college attendance to college credentials at the A.A., B.A., M.A., and Ph.D. levels.

Furthermore, such careers imply the delivery of services to the rich and the middle class as well as to the poor and specific neglected or vulnerable groups in society such as children, the elderly, retarded, disabled, etc. In addition, providers in service careers can be primarily located in the public or private sectors, be involved in treatment or prevention, long-range planning or crisis intervention. I will not attempt to restrict the social service categories in any way but will use the social work master degree programs in my examples. I do urge everyone to make applications to other service careers and programs.

Thirdly, I must say that in view of President Reagan's budgetary policies, the present political climate, and the forceable power of today's so-called moral majority, social service careers and Puerto Rican Studies may be in jeopardy.

Let me briefly elaborate on this third issue. In terms of social service education, Mr. Reagan proposed a $14 million cut in NIMH training for fiscal year 1981; another $13 million cut for 1982. Drug and alcohol programs were to be cut from $13.4 million currently to $13 million in 1981, and further reduced by another $2 million in 1982. Aging training money were to be reduced from $14 million to $12 million, then to $6 million in 1982. Mental and child health social service training and education money would be cut by $5 million for the next fiscal year and still further for 1982. Furthermore, the end of revenue sharing puts an end to undifferentiated services and training funds and gives funds to the states without recalling a "maintenance of effort." In effect this means that states can do just about anything with the funds; hence social service schools are in the position of risking cuts in services if they request funds for social service education.

These cuts, along with the reductions in student support and reduced state budgets, signify a dramatic change in the student body. Eventually, only the more affluent will attain graduate education in social work and other social services, and the limited gains some schools have made in recruiting Puerto Ricans would be ended. This would mean that social service careers would again be the domain of the upper middle class—a time when social services ignored Puerto Ricans and most faculties of social service schools never entertained the notion of a Puerto Rican Studies curriculum.

Let us work to reverse this bleak scenario and examine Puerto Rican Studies curriculum from a historical present and future perspective.

Just what has existed in the past in terms of Puerto Rican Studies and social work education in the United States? To answer that we must consider historical forces impacting on social work in general and on the history of Puerto Ricans in particular.

American society has justified the exploitation of third world people in order to either enslave them, as is the case of Africans, take their land, as in the case of the Mexicans, Native American Indians, and Puerto Ricans, or to maintain a cheap supply of labor as is still very much the case today with Blacks and Puerto Ricans in the northeast. The justification for the exploitation has taken different forms over the centuries. Initially the dominant form of exploitation was brutal and included enslavement and seeing people as property. This was justified by a philosophy which held that Blacks were subhuman, animal like heathens that were better off in bondage than in their native lands.[1]

As time passed and more and more Blacks entered trades and did work which demonstrated a great deal of skills and intelligence the ideology was altered and Blacks were no longer seen as subhuman but as an inferior race. Much of the intellectual thinking for this theory was supplied by Social Darwinists like Spencer. The oppression of Jim Crow laws then had scientific, scholarly support.[2]

It was this ideology—that of white man's burden and manifest destiny which also justified the American take over of Puerto Rico and its expansion into Asia, Latin America, and the Pacific. In reality, according to Maldonado Denis in his book, *Puerto Rico, A Social Cultural Interpretation*, America's move into the Caribbean "was a movement to gain commercial, industrial, and financial hegemony in the Western Hemisphere, and, as a necessary corollary to that, naval and military bases indispensable to maintaining this hegemony.[3] He adds that it is important to note that "the expansion into the Caribbean can not be separated from the expansion toward the Orient, to the Philippines, Hawaii, China, and other countries in search of new markets for its surplus labor."[4]

It was this racist Social Darwinist ideology that permeated the delivery of services at the time that Puerto Ricans began migrating to the United States.

That migration at first is slow and it is not until the 1930s that Puerto Ricans are noticed in New York City. By this time the racist oppressive ideology had again begun shifting from one of subhuman or inferior races to one of cultural disadvantage. Puerto Ricans and other racial minority children of the 1940s, 1950s (and probably still today), grew up hearing that although we were, or are, equal, we are culturally deprived or disadvantaged. It was not our fault—mind you—but it was that we simply had inherited a funny language. Our music was not as good, nor our poetry, nor the way we dress, nor the food we ate, nor the ways we interacted with our parents and family members. Our value system clearly was at best—strange.

This is what I was taught in school either consciously or unconsciously by non-Puerto Rican teachers; social work education and social workers perpetuated that. Even the very few Hispanic social service providers that I remember my friends and relatives discussing always stressed the importance of our becoming more like other Americans. The Children's Aid Society and the Settlement House workers amongst others, used games, trips to museums, and other "culturally enriching activities" to remind us of what they thought we did not have—and to show us our deprivation.

In all fairness to the social work profession—I must add that other professionals we came into contact with were no better. They were usually worse. At least social workers always wanted to know how we felt about everything and showed a great deal of empathy. It is also true that those workers coming into direct contact with us were most often not trained M.S.W.'s. However the M.S.W. workers were usually administrators and supervisors who themselves believed the cultural deprivation theories and who supported the philosophy and orientation of the settlement houses and other service agencies. These agencies were also used to train M.S.W. students. The curriculum at the Schools of Social Work tended not to look at our culture, language, family functions, or traditions as strengths but as different and not as good as the average American's. Attempts to consciously examine cultural differences as such, not as pathology, were minimal. As a result many of our children were pulled out of our homes, were labeled sick or retarded, and often enough the brightest of them were seen as exceptions, turned away from us and encouraged to assimilate into a white American world.

Puerto Rican social workers who attended schools of social work in the 1950s tell me that Puerto Ricans were not looked at as having special needs, problems, or aspirations. Puerto Ricans were usually not discussed at all. The more progressive instructors, when discussing socio-cultural issues used the Jewish community as the example, and at times the Black community. Puerto Rican cases or examples were reviewed if there was a Puerto Rican student in the class who chose to make a presentation using a Puerto Rican person or group as the focus for that presentation.

This pattern was generally true in New York Social Work Schools throughout the 1950s and early 1960s even though according to the U.S. census there were over 615,000 persons of Puerto Rican heritage in New York City by 1960.

Outside New York City, where Puerto Rican communities did not have the strength of numbers, had less political clout, and were not as sophisticated as New York's, schools of social work felt even less need to develop Puerto Rican Studies curricula.

The late 1950s and early 1960s witnessed the creation of some Puerto Rican organizations that stressed the development of second-generation Puerto Ricans, and which argued that we as Puerto Ricans had to form our own groups, and our own social service agencies and institutions. Through such mechanisms, Puerto Rican individuals could voice their concerns and take stands on issues affecting themselves and other Puerto Ricans. Some of these organizations include the Puerto Rican Association for Community Affairs (PRACA), AS-PIRA, and the Puerto Rican Forum. The 1964 Puerto Rican Community Development Project (PRCDP), begun by the Puerto Rican Forum, and whose central staff included Toni Pantoja, Josephine Nieves, Haydee Masso, and myself, undertook the responsibility of pulling together the first composite look of the Puerto Rican community in New York City.

This was the first time that such an effort was controlled by Puerto Ricans. The PRCDP document became the most comprehensive picture of New York City's Puerto Rican population to date. In addition to basic demographic data, PRCDP presented a striving, energetic community. It clearly outlined the Puerto Rican migration as a function of the economic system and stressed the need for self-help organizations and programs to address the problems which Puerto Ricans confronted. Unlike other racial groups, the report concluded, we were scattered throughout the city and would have greater difficulty impacting on any one neighborhood since we did not form a majority in any of the several areas in which we were concentrated. This geographic reality contributed to our political powerlessness. The strongest and most controversial aspect of the report at that time was the incredible amount of documentation which clearly placed Puerto Ricans at the very bottom of New York City's socio-economic ladder. The report also spelled out the reasons why it was probable that we would remain there unless there was massive intervention. The notion that we were like past immigrants and that given sufficient time we would follow the footsteps of past European immigrants was clearly dispelled. We had to identify and compare ourselves not so much to past European immigrants but to the country's racial minorities.

To some Puerto Rican leaders of the time, making such statements was unforgivable—like airing our dirty laundry in public. The horrible picture of poverty was balanced by hope for the future; our sheer numbers and social services which would stress the importance of understanding our lifestyles, history, and culture; this would encourage education, training, employment, and other vehicles for empowerment. The study paved the way for PRCDP to become a full-fledged agency. It also offered support for the idea of a Puerto Rican Family Institute, another effort initiated by Puerto Rican social workers.

Puerto Rican social workers have often led the battle for the creation of services to Puerto Ricans, for the creation of Puerto Rican controlled groups and institutions. Several of us have often been at the forefront of movements such as community control struggles. Social work ideology and values like the client's right to self-determination and much of community organization theory and practice are congruent with the needs of our people. The M.S.W. has at times given some Puerto Ricans the necessary credentials to validate our involvement in planning for and providing services. And indeed, the credentials of the teaching and social work professionals were the ones that we felt we could reasonably aspire to attain. However, social work schools and the social service network themselves have indeed been strangers to us as a people. What we Puerto Rican social workers did in the 1960s was to turn to ourselves for solutions, and solutions often meant creating our own networks for the provision of services and the turning to the political arena.

By the end of the decade the groundwork was set for Puerto Rican social workers and social work students to begin bearing pressure on the universities. This groundwork was coupled with the militancy of the civil rights movement and the realization by the schools of social work of the fact that they were often housed in the middle of Puerto Rican neighborhoods.

And yet when I entered Columbia University School of Social Work in 1966 there was only one Puerto Rican student in the class before mine and four others in my own class. None of us were encouraged to do our field work practice in Puerto Rican settings and Puerto Rican issues were still being discussed only when we raised them. Despite our small numbers Puerto Rican social work students in the late 1960s demanded the introduction of Puerto Rican Studies and Social Work Practice curriculum in several of the New York City Social Work schools. The gains were modest; at best one elective course would be negotiated. Puerto Rican social work students, social workers, and community leaders have continued negotiating with the schools for field instructors, faculty, curriculum, and students.

Response to Puerto Rican negotiating efforts has been sporadic and not tremendously fruitful. However, Puerto Rican agents have been placed before many of the schools throughout the country, in areas of large Puerto Rican populations, and before the National Association of Social Workers (NASW) and the Council of Social Work Education (CSWE). By 1974, according to CSWE statistics Puerto Rican students represented 1.7 percent or 147 students of all second-year M.S.W. students. Let me quickly add that this includes the University of Puerto Rico with its 72 Puerto Rican second-year students. The actual number of Puerto Rican second-year M.S.W. students in 1974 in the U.S. was not 147 but 85. The percentage then, much less than 1 percent. Even that small number, however, is large when compared to the 1940s, 1950s, and even the 1960s. I want to add that the reason for that increase is probably the Open Admissions policy of the City University of New York and the development of Puerto Rican Studies programs on those campuses in the late 1960s and early 1970s.

The number and percentage of full-time Puerto Rican faculty in graduate schools of Social Work in the United States and Puerto Rico in 1974 was 39 or 1.8 percent of all such faculty. Again, eliminating the University of Puerto Rico's 23 members, leaves us with 16 full time Puerto Rican faculty members—once again much less than 1 percent of all graduate schools full-time faculty. In 79 schools of Social Work in the country, out of 2,183 full-time faculty persons, 16 were Puerto Rican in 1974.

Obviously one can not have Puerto Rican Studies Curriculum in Social Services without Puerto Rican students and faculty. It is the presence of Puerto Rican students and faculty that has led to the beginning of Puerto Rican Studies Curriculum in Social Service Schools.

Turning specifically to such curriculum one can generalize that in most schools of social work the Puerto Rican is being looked at in a manner which is very different from the 1950s *West Side Story* approach. And yet, too often, pathology is still the orientation, assimilation the goal. The numbers of Puerto Ricans in social work schools as either students or faculty is minimal. Puerto Ricans are often categorized under the rubric of Blacks and Puerto Ricans—minorities, Hispanics, etc., in curriculum matters. In some schools, courses entitled "The Black Experience & The Experience of Other Racial Minorities," are in some semesters the only required courses that spend any time on Puerto Ricans as culturally, economically, and politically unique people. Several social work schools, like Columbia University, Boston University, Hunter College, Fordham University, and Stony Brook, have or are developing Puerto Rican Studies courses within their social work programs. Perhaps, if there is faculty of such schools present in this workshop, they will volunteer to share their curriculum with us.

I am gong to take the liberty of sharing with you the Puerto Rican Studies Curriculum that two of my colleagues, Migdalia Reyes, Myrna Maldonado McMaster, and I, have developed at the University of Connecticut School of Social Work and for which I requested NIMH funding. This curriculum is part of a larger Puerto Rican Studies Project which I coordinate. The NIMH funded Puerto Rican Studies Project has three general objectives. They are:

1. To develop a comprehensive substantive area (field of concentration) on the delivery of services to Puerto Ricans as part of the master's program at UCSSW.

2. To increase the knowledge base of social service providers (Puerto Rican and non-Puerto Rican) actively involved in servicing Puerto Rican clients and client systems.

This objective is designed to address the lack of knowledge of many providers in the human services field about Puerto Rican culture and its impact on behavior. Based on the assumption that the substantive area would be actively involved in the development of new knowledge, this objective addresses the need to put this knowledge to immediate use in the delivery of services in order to improve services as well as to test the knowledge itself.

3. To increase the number of Puerto Ricans interested in, and entering, social work as a profession in Connecticut. In order to increase the number of Puerto Ricans in service delivery, a two-pronged approach is proposed. First, this project attempts to increase general awareness of social work as a potential profession within the

Puerto Rican community; second, it continues and expands the efforts of the University of Connecticut to recruit Puerto Ricans to its graduate school of Social Work.

At the University of Connecticut the Master of Social Work degree covers two academic years beyond the bachelor's degree. A minimum of 60 credits is required for the degree, including 40 credits of classroom courses and 20 credits in field education. All students must take five required courses, called *school basics*. Students must also concentrate in a social work method: casework, group work, community organization, administration, or policy and planning. A second method is also required. After the required courses and field work credits are added up, a minimum of 14 credits (7 courses) remain. Students may select courses from any of the many electives to complete their 60 credits. The School now offers students the opportunity of taking most or all of their electives in one specific area of concentration or, as we call them, substantive areas. Currently eight substantive areas are in place. They are aging; criminal justice; family and children's services; health; mental health; social and the law; women's issues and social work practice; and as of March 13, 1981 an eighth, Puerto Rican Studies.

There are five approved courses on Puerto Rican Studies at the University of Connecticut School of Social Work (UCSSW). In addition, one of the school's basic courses, required of all students at the UCSSW, entitled Human Oppression, devotes half of the semester to the Puerto Rican Experience.

Please allow me to describe the content of that school basic course and briefly outline the other 5 courses.

The School Basic on Human Oppression

This course places the Puerto Rican Experience within a general framework of oppression. Half of the course content is on The Black Experience, the other half offers salient aspects of Puerto Rican history and culture, discusses the factors leading to the American invasion of Puerto Rico and those explaining the Puerto Rican migration to the United States. It also looks at the diffusion of the Puerto Rican population throughout the United States and explores the role of the social worker *vis-à-vis* his or her Puerto Rican client system.

Students are asked to take this course during their first year so that their exposure to Puerto Rican content may help them request more specifics on working with Puerto Rican client systems in their other courses. The Puerto Rican content of the course is taught by a Puerto Rican faculty member.

The courses which have been developed and which have been or will be offered in the Puerto Rican Studies Substantive Area are:

The Puerto Rican Experience   FIRST COURSE

Course Description

The content of this course expands on the information presented in the Human Oppression basic. It emphasizes Puerto Rico's unique social mixture and resulting cultural, linguistic, religious, and physical blendings. Special attention is given to the industrialization of the Island, the economy in Puerto Rico, migration trends, class and race in Puerto Rico and the United States, and ethnic and racial competition in this country. The course also explores issues related to Puerto Rican poverty and examines the social service delivery network in the United States—specifically the delivery of social services to Puerto Ricans in the State of Connecticut. My doctoral dissertation, *Puerto Rican Poverty and The Migration To Elsewhere,* serves as the basic text for this course. (2 credits)

Socio-Cultural Characteristics of the   SECOND COURSE
Puerto Rican Community and the
Delivery of Social Services

Course Description:

Prerequisite for this course is the Puerto Rican Experience of the Human Oppression School basic. This course examines socio-cultural characteristics which are necessary knowledge in the provision of services to Puerto Rican client systems. The Puerto Rican family, child rearing practices, the oppression of the Puerto Rican Woman, sexual roles, machismo, religious practices (including Pentacostalism and spiritualism) are examined in view of social service delivery in general and health and mental health services specifically. This course highlights cultural strengths and traditional support networks in Puerto Rican communities rather than viewing cultural differences as pathology. (2 credits)

Goals

To provide social work students with a working knowledge of:

a. cultural values

b. attitudes and behavior
c. networks of support
d. practice and techniques of social work intervention with Puerto Rican client systems;

and thus enable future social workers to have a more effective understanding of the Puerto Rican people living in the State of Connecticut.

Social, Economic and Political Issues and Concerns Affecting Puerto Rican Communities **THIRD COURSE**

Course Description

Focusing on macro issues, this course examines the larger societal order and its effects on the lives of Puerto Rican children, families, and communities. Some topics explored are identity, drug abuse, the justice system, employment and unemployment, the educational system, welfare, and housing. An exploration of the interaction between the Puerto Rican people and other systems within the North American society is made. Scholars and community leaders are brought in as lecturers and their presentations are open to the University's general student body, faculty, and greater community.

Course Objectives

To provide social work students with a working knowledge of social, economic and political dynamics and their effects on Puerto Rican client systems.

To examine the social forces and institutions which affect Puerto Rican individuals, families, and communities, and their ability to interact and function in the United States.

To examine current issues which have implications for the future of the Puerto Rican nation.

To examine the attitudes of the students enrolled in the course toward these issues and provide a forum for facilitating growth and change.

To examine possible intervention strategies for combating problems affecting Puerto Rican clients systems.

Research in Puerto Rican Studies

Course Description:

This course will critically examine existing research on Puerto Ricans. It will analyze past research efforts, on Puerto Ricans, reviewing methodology and techniques in connection with application to practical problems and concerns in social work. Working in small groups students will be expected to implement a research study in a selected practice area or problems affecting Puerto Rican client systems. The understanding of all of the factors involved in the research process will be tested as part of the competency requirements for completion of the Puerto Rican Studies Substantive Area. Prerequisite: B-330 (Social Work Research Methodology) and HB-328 (The Puerto Rican Experience).

Course Objectives:

1. To demonstrate to students the paucity of research efforts concentrating on Puerto Rican client systems.
2. To prepare students to be critical of research pertaining to Puerto Ricans and provide techniques for assessing the use of language, cultural, economic, and political relevancy in the research process.
3. To encourage students to become involved in research efforts aimed at understanding and addressing factors impeding Puerto Rican progress and mobility.
4. To help guide students in the Puerto Rican Studies Substantive Area through their competency requirements.

Integrating Seminar on Puerto Rican Studies and Social Work Practice

This seminar will meet every other week for two semesters. It is designed to integrate field education with classroom work. It will also explore approaches to the social problems and issues affecting Puerto Rican client systems, from the perspective of the various social work methods. Required of all students in the Puerto Rican Substantive Area.

Other Requirements

As part of the curriculum in the School a minimum of 4 semesters of field work is required. For students in the Puerto Rican Studies

Substantive Area appropriate field placements in the many Connecticut cities with large Puerto Rican concentrations are selected so that the students' practice will complement the theoretical components offered in the substantive area curriculum. Students in the Puerto Rican Studies Substantive Area will have the opportunity to practice the method of their choice, but must do so with a Puerto Rican client system for at least two consecutive semesters of practice. Because much of the literature and in most cases the client system necessitate fluency in Spanish, Spanish reading and conversation skills are necessary for all students graduating with a Puerto Rican Studies Substantive Area specialization. However, the courses are geared to any student in the M.S.W. program wishing to enroll in them. The Spanish Conversation Course already taught at the School is available for students needing such skills. Summarizing our academic program in Puerto Rican Studies, students who wish to receive a special certificate in the Puerto Rican Studies Substantive Area at the University of Connecticut School of Social Work would have to meet all of the requirements for the M.S.W. degree and in addition would have to complete the following:

1. At least eight credits in course work. The threshold course (The Puerto Rican Experience), Research in Puerto Rican Studies, and the Integrating Seminar are required.
2. At least two consecutive semesters of their field education must be related to the substantive work.
3. A demonstration of reading and conversation skills in the Spanish language.
4. A demonstration of competency upon completion of all other requirements.

Grassroot organizations often do not have professionally trained social workers on their staff and are at times not in the position to accept M.S.W. trainees. The Puerto Rican Studies Project makes this arrangement more possible by allowing school personnel to act as field supervisors and consultants in such agencies.

Let me end by stating that all of our Puerto Rican Studies curricula contain some very basic themes. Advocating for, and with, Puerto Rican client systems, historical and cultural awareness, commitment to social change, egalitarianism, support for the eradication of sexism, racism, homophobia, ageism, and discrimination against the disabled, awareness of the colonial status of Puerto Rico, the importance of coalition building, are some themes that come readily to my mind.

Obtaining this program has not been easy. There have been budgetary problems and it has taken a great deal of time and energy and commitment on the part of the Puerto Rican Studies faculty and Puerto Rican and Hispanic students. The program was conceived and developed by me, although I was hired to teach community organization, social welfare planning, and other courses—not to start a Puerto Rican Studies Project. In other words, putting it mildly this Project was not a School priority. We have sought and obtained a great deal of support from the Women's Student Organization, the Lesbian and Gay Alliance, the Disabled Students, the Black Student Organization, progressive faculty, and the administration of the School of Social Work. Without a doubt my activist background, numerous administrative positions at the School (such as being chairman of a department), organization and negotiation skill, and academic credentials have been helpful. A bright and dedicated faculty, an increasing Puerto Rican student body, and NIMH funding has also facilitated this effort.

The program is still new and far from perfect. It may not be easily replicable in a less progressive atmosphere, especially as a result of the political climate I stressed earlier.

I do want to again emphasize that the curriculum in the Puerto Rican Studies course is part of a larger project. . . We work very hard on conferences, workshops, seminars, and other structured and unstructured activities to raise the consciousness of the entire social work community. We very actively recruit students and become involved in community work. We are planning a social work journal that will address issues affecting Puerto Ricans.

We believe that social service providers are in an excellent position to help people understand their troubles, not solely from the prevalent pathology model, but from one that describes and analyzes present society as greatly contributing to the creation of that pathology. Grier and Cobbs, in *Black Rage*, state that it is possible for social service providers to be very political. They say, "Let us enter a plea for clinicians who can distinguish unconscious depression from conscious desperation, paranoia from adaptive wariness, and who can tell the difference between a sick mind and a sick nation." Puerto Rican Studies must contribute to exposing this nation's sickness.

Puerto Rican Studies curricula, as I defined in my introduction, must be political. Knowledge and skills by themselves are not enough. Puerto Rican social service providers must become involved in advocacy for Puerto Ricans and other exploited groups and in the broader struggle for human liberation and societal change.

Notes

1. See, Richard Hofstader, *Social Darwinism In American Thought.* Philadelphia: University of Pennsylvania Press, 1944.

2. *Ibid.*

3. Manuel Maldonado Denis. *Puerto Rico: A Socio-Historical Interpretation.* New York: Random House, 1972, p. 67.

4. *Ibid.*

PART THREE

THE RESPONSE TO THE CHALLENGES OF PUERTO RICAN STUDIES

13

Puerto Rican Studies and Continuing Adult Education: Reflections on General Education

Patrick J. Hill

We would all acknowledge, I trust, that undergraduate education is in shambles. The widespread concern for general education is one of the few public acknowledgements of this shambles. While diverse approaches to reconstruction and the myriad private visions of the future are in some important sense a function of that sorry state, we can nonetheless derive mutual benefit from a hard-nosed reflection on our diverse experiences.

Academically disinherited students and traditional faculty bring radically mismatched expectations to the classroom. In brief, the students expect: 1. an imaginable link between courses of study and their post-baccalaureate lives; 2. the opportunity to evolve personal and social direction for their lives in their courses of study; 3. face-to-face interchange with faculty based on the students' own ideas; and 4. faculty initiative and leadership in the process of education. Faculty expect: a. their primary business is research and the sharing of results; b. good students will willingly participate in faculty-initiated inquiries; and c. good teaching is, by and large, identified with the best possible presentation of the most recently researched material.

These mismatched expectations evolve rather rapidly into the situation of mutual withdrawal from responsibilities. Students and faculty are so disappointed with the performance of each other that means are found to minimize conflict and even to avoid interaction. Needless to say, the consequences for the quality of education are disastrous.

New students are overwhelmed by the institution of higher education and find it unintelligible. Many dimensions of this unintelligibility can be enumerated, most important of which are the following: 1. the size and complexity of the institution; 2. the unmanageability of knowledge—no institutional principle of selection is operative to assist students in separating out what is more important from what is less important; 3. the highly specialized nature of disciplinary research and departmental offerings; 4. the remoteness of much of the academic enterprise from the students' experience; 5. centralized and bureaucratic administrative procedures; and 6. most of all, the atomized nature of the course offerings—no visible relationship exists between the courses and the professors, forcing each course to stand on its own, thereby reducing all intellectual matters to matters of taste.

In the atomized curriculum all academic relationships are reduced to one-on-one encounters of faculty and students. There is no common or shared experience, no public dimension to academic enterprise. Students are deprived of the stimulus of an engaging and diverse academic community. The environment is constructed as if we believed that leaving people alone is the most sacred of educational principles.

The above problems might have been addressed as if they were problems of internal management of higher education. Much of general education seems to respond to these problems in solely those terms. At Stony Brook, the problems were seen not only as internal management problems but also as reflections of the shattering of the cultural synthesis of the West which dates back to Descartes. That synthesis can be characterized in terms of scientism, rationalism, high technology, secularization, atomistic intellectualism, and centralized bureaucratic structures. A host of recently emerging problems, e.g., the environmental crisis, the proliferation of nuclear arms, and the decay of cities, constitute a new and complex world that cannot be managed nor even understood by the dominant intellectual paradigms.

Obviously, this understanding of our times precluded a merely internal response. Not so obviously, it precluded our conceiving the major need in the terms familiar to the general education movement, namely those of consolidation and commonality. In a culture that is unraveling and groping for new patterns of intelligibility, the principal task is not to affirm what is common, rather, it is to create structures— curricular structures—of association and invention and discovery and coherence. If successful, these structures would enable insights into our fragmented disciplines, our subcultures, and our ideologies to sustain dialogue with each other about the nature of the world we must create. The desideratum, more concretely speaking, would be to create curricular structures in which sustained dialogue is made possible and visible between the sciences and the humanities, between the feminine and masculine understanding of what it means to be human, between the differing priorities of the generations, between subcultures still in close touch with their pre-industrial roots, and with the fading industrial model of society. The expectation, of course, would not be that one model would triumph over another, but rather as Socrates expected amidst the collapse of Athenian civilization, that only in the pooling of our diverse experiences will the new paradigm emerge. One may refer to Denis Goulet writing about the dialogue between first world and third world countries: "Wisdom for our times can only emerge from creative dialogue—conducted in the mode of reciprocity—between 'old' and 'new' societies. Such reciprocity can only be achieved if all patterns of domination, cultural no less than economic, are abolished."[1] Relative to the invention and discovery of a new cultural paradigm, our students are not merely passive participants in the process—they are resources and coinventors. As some Christian missionaries in Africa have finally learned to start with the experience and wisdom embodied in African proverbs and have learned thereby to expect that their own understanding of the gospels will be transformed in dialogue, so we, too, as educators must develop means by which the experience and the values of the next generation can contribute productively to the dialogue about the emerging new paradigm. The skills possessed by the ideal graduate, those in terms of which the generally educated person would be defined, are those appropriate to building and sustaining and con-tributing to a diverse democratic community grappling with the major issues of our times. Educated persons of this mold are accomplished in one discipline and understand its strengths and weaknesses, most particularly the inherent partiality of its viewpoint. They have moved from passivity to active moral commitment in a relativistic world; they have immersed themselves in a communal, interdisciplinary study of one problem of social magnitude; they have learned thereby the value, indeed, the necessity, of seeking many and diverse perspectives; they have developed skills in understanding and in integrating these diverse perspectives; they have mastered the systems of access to those perspectives; they will themselves be able to conduct with their colleagues and to contribute their own expertise to subsequent social issues as the need arises in their lives. Tolerance of ambiguity, empathic understanding, a sense of partiality, openness to growth through dialogue in plural communities—all those things have become so important to them that a communal inquiry is a major source of joy in their lives. Educational contexts or media can be created in which specialization need not mean narrowness or lack of generality. Atom-ized specialization is educationally dysfunctional, leading as it does to exaggerated and obtuse claims, self-deception and contextual in-sensitivity. In the atomistic context, excessive specialization is a cognitive deformity. But specialization in a richly interactive community is a different cognitive species. So different is it in fact, that the context enables us to see some things about specialization that have been long hidden by the atomistic curriculum, *viz.*, that specialization is not only good but it is a natural starting point of inquiry. To be, to have a perspective, to be located, to be partial. Cognitive, psychological, social, and educational harm results not from the partiality of specialization but from the socially atomistic curriculum and culture which effectively insulates specialized individuals from each other and sets each up as an unquestioned arbiter in a private classroom. In real community, the meaning of specialization is transformed.

Specialization, I repeat, is a natural starting point. I would by no means rule out the desirability of transcending that starting point to develop human beings with more stereoscopic vision or protean consciousness. But one might, with little cognition, lose focus instead of developing human beings with a sense of their own partiality and of the necessity of supplementing that partiality in pluralistic communities.

The last implication for the general education movement can be framed in terms of the Dewey-Hutchins debate which is very instructive, but not one that requires an either-or choice. Like most philosophical debates, each side has hold of one part of a more comprehensive truth: in this case, we are all human beings *and* every version of being human is uniquely different. In higher education, I believe, we have oscillated between these two views, emphasizing at one time what we have in common and at another what makes us different. Curricular structures with required courses of Black and Puerto Rican Studies departments spring up as one or the other is emphasized. The real task is to create curricular structures which are open to both the universal and the unique dimensions of being human; and to place those dimensions in dialogue with each other.

Notes

1. Denis Goulet, "A Summary Statement," *Review of Social Economy,* September 1968, p. 120.

14
Puerto Rican Studies and Community Activism in the 1980s

James Jennings

In a recent study Faustine Jones describes how American society is moving toward the 'Right' of the political spectrum.[1] She points out that in the arena of politics, economics, and education a commitment to equal opportunities is rapidly eroding in America. Jones would have been slightly more accurate if she had argued, not that America is moving toward the Right but rather that American society is returning to "normalcy," after a brief hiatus of liberalism. We live in a society where Puerto Ricans, as well as Blacks, have not been allowed to move beyond poverty during any period of its history. Yes, some individuals have made it (even this can be debated when we look at the basis of this individual progress, however), but for the masses of Puerto Ricans the reality is one of political, economic, and educational depression. This is not new; Puerto Ricans have, in effect, been rejected by the United States since this group first came to this country in significant numbers. What is new, however, is the worsening situation of Puerto Ricans in the U.S. As one indication of this deterioration, note that in 1959 it was reported that 28 percent of all Puerto Ricans had incomes under the poverty level; in 1974 this figure climbed to 33 percent; and in 1979 it increased further to 39 percent.[2]

Various explanations for the state of socio-economic depression in the Puerto Rican communities can be offered. We can debate these explanations and also argue whether poor life conditions are an intentional or unintentional result of various kinds of public policies. But the bottom line, the indisputable fact, is that Puerto Ricans do not enjoy the standard of living realized by significant proportions of white Americans. This means that housing is significantly worse for Puerto Ricans than for other groups; it means that quality educational and recreational services are not as available to this group as it is for "mainstream" Americans; it means that our children do not have the opportunities for social, psychological, and physical growth that other Americans enjoy. Once this fact of Puerto Rican life in the U.S. is realized, a major role of Puerto Ricans Studies becomes quite clear. In order to teach about the experiences of Puerto Ricans in American society one requires an understanding of the Puerto Rican community outside the University. But the approach toward Puerto Rican and poor communities cannot be "colonial" or "exploitive." Students should not be sent into Puerto Rican and poor communities merely to extract information. The relationship between Puerto Rican Studies and Puerto Ricans in the ghettos of America must be symbiotic; the link should be mutually beneficial to the student and the community. This can only occur if Puerto Rican Studies uses its resources to change the life conditions not only of the Puerto Rican, but also of other poor communities. A major function for Puerto Rican Studies in the 1980s is to develop concepts, models, and eventually programs which seek to eradicate inequality in American society. Other educational foci must still be pursued within this context. Studies in Puerto Rican culture, literature, history are vitally important for Puerto Ricans and others; but the attempt to involve Puerto Rican Studies in the molding of Puerto Rican communities must be a major one for several reasons.

First of all, Puerto Rican communities in American society reflect unique socio-historical processes; there is much ignorance and misinformation about the socio-economic and historical nature of Puerto Rican communities. As Hernández pointed out in his presentation, we must re-evaluate the utility of accepted traditional social science research concepts when we attempt to investigate the Puerto Rican experience in the United States. For this reason, the information which we compile will have to be based on various kinds of relationships between Puerto Rican Studies on the campus, and the outside community. Other "traditional" departments in the university may not have to rely on this kind of approach for any number of reasons; but for Puerto Rican Studies to have validity, it must provide a channel by which to develop linkages with various sectors of Puerto Rican communities.

Second, generally speaking, academia has not opted to confront the problems which affect Puerto Ricans in this country. In some instances, as a matter of fact, academia has aligned itself with interest groups insensitive to the problems of poverty and inequality. Scholars have been recruited by the private and public sector to justify a *status quo* which is economically smothering Puerto Rican and poor communities. Puerto Rican Studies can adopt investigative activities which examine the assumptions and concepts regarding Puerto Rican communities and basically used to justify the *status quo* of wealth, power, and influence.

Third, Puerto Ricans bring a rich and marvelous culture to American society. This culture cannot grow or be useful if it is not recognized as a community resource and source of group strength. But culture cannot be adequately studied through the mere discussion of things past. The history of Puerto Rican people must be intertwined with the everyday routines of Puerto Ricans; Puerto Rican Studies is in a potentially influential position to create this kind of matrix.

The fourth reason is more purely organizational. Unless Puerto Rican Studies nurtures links with the nonacademic Puerto Rican community, it will not survive on the campus. Advocates for Puerto Rican Studies should seek to develop alliances with the external community; this linkage will be beneficial to the college. Broad-minded administrators will realize that the university must remain accessible to all groups in American society; by developing this linkage Puerto Rican Studies can assist the university in this endeavor.

The process of linkage with the nonacademic Puerto Rican community can occur in various ways. These include three general approaches:

- Research
- Praxis-oriented education in the classroom
- Resource-sharing

A major question affecting Puerto Rican (and poor) communities is the nature of the "urban crisis." This refers to the conglomeration of poverty-related problems we see in various sectors of American cities. Some social scientists have argued that the government should, one, not attempt to solve this urban crisis; or, two, that government is not capable of solving the urban crisis. Either claim leads to public policy frameworks embodying the "benign neglect" concept.[3] There are a number of assumptions associated with this kind of public policies directed at the Puerto Rican community. Puerto Rican Studies conceivably could sponsor research which only seeks to test the assumptions which mold public policy, but also, where necessary, offer alternative ideas for the development of effective public policy in Puerto Rican communities.

Linkage could also be developed through "praxis-oriented education." This approach entails three successive components:

Phase I   Utilization of rigorous theoretical analysis to study various
           kinds of problems in Puerto Rican or poor communities.
           Courses are organized around major economic, political,
           educational, or social problems. Students are encouraged
           to investigate three problems through extensive readings,
           discussions, lecturers, etc.

Phase II   After the first phase is completed students develop
           fieldwork projects which would allow them to volunteer
           free time to a community organization, or to individuals
           working on the kinds of problems investigated during
           Phase I.

Phase III The student plans and completes a comprehensive re-
           search project which focuses on the work in Phase II.
           The research paper should be useful not only to the
           student, but very importantly, useful to the community
           organization or group which sponsored the student.

University resources can be shared with the Puerto Rican community
in a number of ways. These could include informational workshops
or forums, free "courses" on various topics could be offered; for
example, the Puerto Rican public might be interested in registering
for "modules" on Puerto Rican history or politics. Some persons
might register for a one-day course on the effects of "Reaganomics,"
still others might feel a need for career-related information.

This essay does not seek to proffer what the structural format of
Puerto Rican Studies might be on a college campus. Instead, it
concentrates on the advocacy of an educational philosophy which
calls for linkage between Puerto Rican Studies and the Puerto Rican
community outside academia. This may not be only philosophical
orientation embodied in Puerto Rican Studies, but it should be a
major one. The ideas offered here may take various organizational
formats, depending on a number of factors. These include the size
of the faculty associated with Puerto Rican Studies, whether it is a
program or a department, the pool of available students and their
interests, the ways in which curriculum is determined, perhaps the
location of the college or university, and no doubt there are other
considerations.

Many of the statements included here are not new; these ideas
have been discussed in many circles over the last fifteen years or so.
But Faustine Jones is correct in suggesting that American society is
moving toward a direction which bodes ill for those without power
or wealth. During this period of re-emerging conservatism the direction
that Puerto Rican Studies can or should take, especially in regards

to the life conditions found in Puerto Rican ghettos, will be of vital importance.

Notes

1. Faustine Jones, *Changing Mood in America: Eroding Commitment?* (Howard University Press: Washington, D.C., 1977).

2. Kal Wagenheim, *A Survey of Puerto Ricans in the U.S. Mainland in the 1970's* (Praeger Publishers: New York, 1976); also, see, *Social Indicators of Equality for Minorities and Women: A Report of the U.S. Commission on Civil Rights* (August 1978).

3. This suggests that the problems of racial and ethnic minorities are beyond the control of governmental politics. Owing to family disorganization, psychological or cultural disadvantages some ethnic groups will not be able to "catch up" with white Americans, and, therefore, governmental activism in this regard is futile. The phrase itself was suggested by Daniel Patrick Moynihan in 1971 while serving as an advisor to President Richard Nixon.

EPILOGUE

Toward a Renaissance of Puerto Rican Studies: An Essay of Redefinition

Antonio M. Stevens-Arroyo

It ought to be said at the onset, that using the word "renaissance" in reference to Puerto Rican Studies is an attempt at analogy. The original Renaissance was a transition stage from the Medieval World to the Enlightenment, and any contemporary renaissance will be a period of change from one circumstance to another. To speak of a renaissance of Puerto Rican Studies, then is to find a basis for comparing our present situation with an epoch that rediscovered social and cultural paradigms for an emerging new historical reality.

The most extensive part of this book quite properly has been devoted to detailed statements about distinct facets of Puerto Rican Studies. Can these insights be understood as new paradigms of thought and expression? Are we presented today with an emerging new historical reality? Are Puerto Rican Studies applicable to the challenges before us? These questions must be explored before it can be said that Puerto Rican Studies is undergoing a renaissance.

Rediscovery of a Cultural Matrix

Puerto Rican Studies in the City University of New York (CUNY) arose from controversy. The militancy and political adroitness of Black and Puerto Rican students and a handful of faculty in the agitated days of 1968–69 forced CUNY administrators to concede to these articulate groups the opportunity to shape academic programs and departments. But CUNY's administration simultaneously offered to other groups similar opportunities to fashion area and ethnic studies within the university, although such an addition was not a part of the vision of the Black and Puerto Rican militants. It may be said that in this way CUNY saved face before the public. By instituting programs of "ethnic enrichment," the university administration disguised a surrender of the minority peoples of color. The success of militants who forced academia to include the perspective of the oppressed in the curriculum and to allow a greater number of minorities to occupy faculty and administration posts was downplayed in favor of an official version that described the concessions as indications of CUNY's liberalism. Thus, Puerto Rican Studies was born with mixed blessings: the birthright of the barricades gave the fledgling programs a sense of power, but the pairing with ethnic studies reduced what had been an issue of class struggle to one of cultural sensitivity. This is the context for Josephine Nieves' statement that "the institutionalization of Puerto Rican Studies has been both a victory and a defeat."

Ambiguity about the creation of Puerto Rican Studies continues to plague us today. Administrators past and present generally have tended to perceive Puerto Rican Studies as part of the ethnic studies paradigm. In this model, the university allows cultural pluralism within the gamut of the traditional curriculum in order to offer students a sense of identity and to showcase the city's cultural, racial, and religious diversity. Worship at the shrine of liberalism eventually produced Italian-American, Asian-American, Irish-American, and similar hyphenated "American" studies that have come to occupy equal ground with Puerto Rican Studies. By ignoring the ugly effects of racism, imperialism, and social class oppression, justice was reduced by the administration to a set of well-meaning intentions. To be "sensitive" or "aware" of cultural difference made one a practioner of cultural pluralism. Even if the injustice persisted, those who had become sensitized were excused from culpability for the inequalities of social power that prevailed in society in general and the university in particular.

In the past ten years, cultural pluralism has prevailed as an ideology for much of the U.S. society. Joshua Fishman comments that "the new ethnicity is . . . at home with America," and he adds, "It claims that if America is any good at all, any better at all than the purported bad guys elsewhere, then it should value ethnicity, protect ethnicity, develop ethnicity, foster ethnicity, particularly ethnicity X that has contributed so much to the poetry, music, wit, wisdom, humor, and gentleness of life in this world and the next. . . . The rejection and degradation of ethnicity led to a decline and fall of America. The revival and re-enthronement of ethnicity will lead to America's rise and shine!" While Fishman finds this ideology "overly simple and overly brash," he nonetheless asserts that it is "revivalistic, messianistic, and powerfully moving."[1]

On the premise that all groups ought to receive equal opportunity within society, supporters of the new ethnicity supported bilingual education and affirmative action programs of all types. This premise of cultural pluralism was congenial to Puerto Rican Studies, perhaps, because with so many doors being opened without confrontation, the more radical class and radical issues appeared to be unnecessary polemics. Whatever the reasons, it was only at times of crisis—such as the attempt at Brooklyn College in 1974–75 to impose a chairperson on the department—that the original militancy was summoned up in order to confront a university administration. On the whole, cultural pluralism was viewed as an ideology favorable to maintaining a Puerto Rican presence within the university.

These observations about the differences between cultural pluralism and the radical commitment that launched Puerto Rican Studies more than a decade ago are relevant to the assessment of our fidelity to our origins. Cultural pluralists may or may not agree with the long-range purposes of Puerto Rican Studies, they may or may not be allies within the university—what is crucial, however, is the impact they have had on our self-perceptions and our goals. As Jose Hernández wrote a decade ago, these cultural pluralists perceive the Puerto Rican struggle as "some sort of learning process or socialization to the new environment, generally beginning wih the letter 'A'—accommodation, adjustment, assimilation, acculturation, amalgamation."[2] All of these trends can be subsumed under the "big 'A'" of Americanization. The brave Puerto Rican students and educators who had risked and often sacrificed their careers in order to gain a foothold in the university system looked beyond cultural sensitivity in their struggles. They sought power and participation in order to change things, while "the system" made concessions in order to maintain the *status quo*. Puerto Rican Studies launched both an academic guerrilla war for radical change in the university as well as an effort to make Puerto Ricans conform to the system by domesticating them and their values. Thus, alongside "conflict" went "mainstreaming," "participation in decision-making" accompanied "control of our own affairs." The seductions of cultural pluralism made the successes of Puerto Rican Studies temptations toward cooptation.

These conflicting perspectives on Puerto Rican Studies have invaded the thinking of Puerto Ricans themselves. The militant struggle for a Puerto Rican difference is frequently counterposed to professionalism. Thus, what was originally a contradiction between our own view of things and the way others saw us sometimes became our own brand of schizophrenia. We want to preserve our militancy, but to also be respected within the system at the same time. Because we often perceive these goals to be two different masters, not a few Puerto Ricans in the university have come to experience an inner conflict: Are we to spend time preparing articles for scholarly publications or advance the communitarian struggle against the dominant culture's values system? Josephine Nieves posed the dilemma in terms of accountability. According to her, Puerto Rican Studies have come to respond more directly to the demands of the university than to the needs of the community.

There is not enough space in this essay to decide such an issue. But it ought to be clear that while the dilemma is not a false one, the opposition between professional competency and militant commitment is not irreconcilable. If—and it is a big "if"—what we do well for the sake of our students and people were ever to be accepted as meritorious credentials for university life, then we would simultaneously satisfy both sets of goals.

There are grounds to believe that we are now in a sort of transition stage between the complete incompatibility of these goals and their definitive reconciliation. The grounds for this optimism rest upon the gradual rediscovery of the reasons for the original militancy. We can now translate what was our moral outrage at injustice into a conceptual articulation of our place in the scheme of things. I believe that the people in Puerto Rican Studies are fashioning a clearer expression of what we are all about. The more clearly we know what we stand for, the less shrill will be our denunciation of what we are against. This is not meant to suggest that we were unclear about our purposes in the past, but simply to assert that in the passage of time we have been offered a new context in which to make ourselves better understood by others.

An example of this new context of Puerto Rican Studies is the way Puerto Rican migration to the United States is treated. The introduction to the Centro's *Labor Migration Under Capitalism* notes, the first migration studies "tended to treat the appearance of Puerto Ricans as just another wave in a steady process of incorporating newly arrived minorities into North American society"; critiques by Puerto Rican scholars frequently "fell short of the mark by failing to provide an alternative analytic approach capable of adequately accounting for the diversity of situations that imprint a particular character on migration in Puerto Rican history."[3]

Because of the Centro's work and the effort by other fine scholars, Puerto Ricans can speak of the migration toward the United States in terms that reject the unidimensional approaches of the past. In the process, we have also made ourselves relevant to students of contemporary Caribbean, Mexican, and even European migration. Puerto Rican migration studies today allow for distinctions of type and numbers, for inclusion of political and economic forces, and for macroeconomic analysis of a new world economic order. This type of development for Puerto Rican migration studies is also enriching aspects of Puerto Rican literature, history, and community studies.

If one had to put a label on these positive development in Puerto Rican Studies it would be "contextualization." We now communicate a more rich perception of our particularity because we can express it in reference to more general realities that affect other people as well. The need for contextualization has been felt before as Gamaliel Perez attests when he complained that it was difficult to project a genuine Puerto Rican Studies agenda without constant reference not only to the United States, but also to Latin America.[4] Today, we are likely to find that recent scholarship has made such comparisons easier.

Unfortunately, this movement toward contextualization has been an uneven process. Not everyone or every field of Puerto Rican Studies has had the benefit of the substantive kind of study provided by the Centro. Often enough, the increasing number of non-Puerto Rican Hispanic students in CUNY classes—e.g., Dominicans, Colombians, and Ecuadorians—has necessitated a wider field of reference for the competent educator. These students often take Puerto Rican Studies' courses because they perceive our programs as the only reliable source of education about Latin America. But however genuine their interest in Puerto Rico, such students are likely to be in search of information about their own countries as well. While in some institutions such as Hostos Community College, the Puerto Rican Studies Department has been redefined to include Latin American Studies, contexualization of this sort generally represents a new challenge to the definition of Puerto Rican Studies. It is not enough to make Puerto Rican Studies the repository for homeless Latin American courses, unless such adaptations assist in the task of contextualization.

Why is it, we should ask, that a fundamental issue like Puerto Rican self-determination is so generally ignored by the university? Support for racial equality, guilt over the holocaust of Jews by the Nazis, and repudiation of the KKK are causes reverenced by the university administration and faculty. But few defend Puerto Rican self-determination and independence with equal fervor. In fact, some perceive this as a "political issue" for those living on the Island to decide. It is not uncommon to hear from the same sources that struggles for self-determination distract Puerto Ricans from the attention due the improvement of their life in the United States. We must admit, I'm afraid, that what is unique to our Puerto Rican situation—colonialism—is generally not understood by the university nor by the larger community. Our inability to explain this issue to others is a sign that we have not yet achieved contextualization in a full and complete way.

It must be recognized that we have frequently accepted the cultural pluralism model. And although it might have entered through the back door of expediency when departments and programs were forced into survival tactics, there can be little progress toward more ambitious projects until we have neutralized this liberal hex.

Cultural pluralism has been pernicious to Puerto Rican Studies because it puts our people into the category of those who need one of the "A's" mentioned above. We are compared individually and as a group to ethnic groups that "made it." Vestiges of our cultural persistence are therefore viewed as pathological attachment to outmoded values. Administration is always "giving us things" (on the assumption that we could not have earned distinction on our own merits). A professionally competent faculty member is held to be untypical of Puerto Rican Studies Departments. We are always to be found on one or other college committee as the "token minority," or as what Clara Rodriguez called "the unpaid Puerto Rican consultant."

Unfortunately, much of the typical Puerto Rican Studies curriculum reflects the cultural pluralism model. The basic courses for Puerto Rican Studies came from a social worker and/or bilingual educator's requisite classes: The Puerto Rican Family, the Puerto Rican Community in New York, Bilingualism and the Puerto Rican Child, etc. These courses, which emphasized the problematic dimensions of the Puerto Rican experience, often pre-existed the founding of Puerto Rican Studies, and had served not only Puerto Rican students, but non-Hispanics interested in social work and/or education. With the opportunity to create a Puerto Rican Studies program of study, came the need to amplify these central "problematic" courses. A curriculum in the mold of "ethnic studies" was added in order to offer classes on the history, culture, politics, and literature of the homeland. Whereas New York-based Puerto Ricans had taught the first set of courses, faculty from Puerto Rico were usually the best equipped professionally to teach the second set of courses.

The two different perspectives—that of the city-based Puerto Rican activist and that of the Island professor—produced its share of unevenness, as others in this volume have pointed out. But while this problem has generally been overcome during the present decade, the double vision of two communities, with two sets of different problems, and two distinct intellectual perspectives, has endured. Although the tone of our courses usually represents the need for radical social change and a challenge to colonialism, the format for the curriculum of Puerto Rican Studies has been cast in the cultural pluralism model.

For instance, the description of courses in Puerto Rican Studies often projects a dichotomy between Puerto Ricans in the states and those on the Island. Curriculum often suggests that one can best understand Puerto Ricans in the United States by studying the rural, traditional culture of the Island. Such a premise ignores the reality that a new generation in Puerto Rico is completely urbanized and that most Puerto Ricans in the United States have been born here and usually have English as their first language. There is need to redesign curriculum so that this serious conceptual problem can be removed from the description of our courses and programs. The alternative is to allow the cultural pluralism premise of gradual assimilation to prevail, reducing Puerto Ricans in the United States to the hyphenated Americans of ethnic studies.

Another flaw of some of the Puerto Rican Studies curriculum is the result of overlap and changing social problems. Not infrequently, professors find themselves asked to teach one course on "study of the organization and functioning of the Puerto Rican community" in New York and another on "analysis of the Puerto Rican experience in New York." One could easily offer the same classes interchangeably in the two courses. The course materials may also be overly narrow and focused on issues that are no longer relevant. At Brooklyn College, for instance, the curriculum offered a course on "the Welfare Rights Movement"—something that has disappeared along with the War on Poverty. This kind of overlap and anachronism is often found in other fields of study as well, reflecting the accumulation of "pet courses" by succeeding waves of faculty. In the case of Puerto Rican Studies, however, the elimination of these defects in curriculum design is likely to require a rediscovery of the purpose and thrust of the department and the program.

This redesign of curriculum is not simply a matter of adding catchy titles to traditional offerings. The purpose is not increased FTE's, not to afford a club for the culturally homesick nor to offer a parallel counseling service to Spanish-speaking remedial students. Our task is to transmit what is understood about the Puerto Rican reality and explore the changing dimensions of what is to be transmitted. While we have not always overcome our limitations, we have gone beyond a one-dimensional insistence on our uniqueness and can now compare our particularity with universal experiences. There is hope that we can build on our small successes and extend the contextualization of Puerto Rican Studies to the whole curriculum.

Reagan's assent to power in 1980 and the revocation by the New Right of cultural pluralism's hegemony makes the task of contextualization all the more urgent. Ironically, the assault upon cultural pluralism may prove a blessing in disguise. Precisely because the liberal premises of academia are under scrutiny, new alliances, coalitions, and reformulations of purpose are more likely than before. In such an intellectual atmosphere, class analysis may come into a sharper focus within scholarly university circles.

Coalition-building or class analysis is not the same as reductionism, however. At times, one would be led to believe that "Puerto Rican" and "proletariat" were interchangeable terms, or that Puerto Ricans were little more than Spanish-speaking blacks. While it is undeniably true that we share most of the oppression of blacks in this country, we have a different historical and cultural past. Just as we try to avoid being lumped together with the Italian-American and Irish-American type of ethnic studies, we have to go beyond an interpretation of the Puerto Rican reality exclusively in racial terms.

Finally Chicano Studies should be considered. Even though we are separated by most of the continent—our programs are concentrated in CUNY and Chicano Studies departments in the California systems—we probably have more in common with each other culturally and ideologically than with Black and ethnic studies. One of the principal fruits of a Brooklyn College conference in 1981 was to have brought representatives of Chicago Studies around the country into contact with Puerto Rican Studies. Whether this encounter will have a long-range effect on Puerto Rican Studies is hard to judge, but recent professional conferences such as the 1983 LASA meeting in Mexico City, have produced panels that allowed for a comparison of Chicano and Puerto Rican topics in history and community development within a United States' context. A 1982 Ford Foundation-funded study highlighted the need to develop curriculum which explains "the historical and juridical facts supporting the claims to language rights and cultural continuity."[5] If this recommendation is extended to literature, art, dance, and music as well as political and cultural movements, the contextualization of Puerto Rican Studies with Chicano experience may be underway. Such efforts, one hopes, will become systematized and strengthened by institutional cooperation, such as is promised by the Centro's participation in projects with Chicano Studies institutes.

In sum, the contextualization of Puerto Rican Studies is a healthy development that has brought us to a threshold of a new understanding of our curriculum and our purposes. But the insights provided us must likely be refined in a thorough curriculum redesign. In that process, the search for Chicanos for many of the same things can be a valuable asset.

The Contemporary Reality

It is commonplace to say that college students in the 1980s are different from their counterparts in the late days of 1968–69, but there is not always hard scientific data to support well-founded assertions about these differences. Fortunately, 1981 and 1982 saw the appearance of two important reports focused upon Puerto Ricans, blacks, and other minorities in higher education. The national survey by the Commission on the Higher Education of Minorities has been referred to above (HEM); the second, issued by the Office of the Deputy Chancellor of CUNY, is entitled *Outcomes of Educational Opportunity: A Study of Graduates from the City University* (OEO).[6] While neither of these documents registers the effect of cutbacks to education owing to economic recession and the Reagan Administration, both carry statistics that make it possible to make some informed statements about Puerto Ricans and Hispanics in CUNY and their relationships to national averages from 1970 until 1979. These statistics also reflect the performance of the majority of Puerto Rican students enrolled at universities with departments or programs of Puerto Rican Studies. Few of the private schools in the city have autonomous Puerto Rican Studies program. Additionally, CUNY accounts for more than half of all the baccalaureate degree conferred in New York City and two-thirds of the associate degrees. Thus, CUNY is not only the sponsor of most of the country's Puerto Rican Studies programs and departments, it also graduates more Puerto Ricans than any other institutions in the country.

The number of minorities in higher education nationwide was at its peak from 1973 until 1977. In CUNY, because of the imposition of tuition in 1975, the "glory years" were gone shortly after they arrived. Nonetheless, OEO shows that Hispanics were 9.7 percent of CUNY enrollment for fall 1975, the last year without tuition, and represented 10 percent of Baccalaureate graduates in June 1979, the normal date for class. The pattern for Hispanics in CUNY community colleges, however, shows no basic difference from blacks.[7]

Four-year college minority students get good marks. The CUNY report showed that the grade point average for minority baccalaureate students had 31.6 percent of students with a 3.00—3.49 index and 18.2 percent 3.5—4.00. Consequently, nearly half of CUNY minority students in four-year college are getting A's and B's.[8] Moreover, roughly the same number of minority students require no remedial course hours.[9] Community college students do not fare as well in either category.

The CUNY report substantiates things already well known, *viz.*, that most of our students are women;[10] that minority people in college tend to be older than the general university student.[11] In CUNY, 20 percent of minority students are married before obtaining their degree; 18 percent have children and hold jobs while studying.[12] It demonstrates that 10 percent of Puerto Rican freshmen in 1981 were single parents or heads of households;[13] one-third contributed weekly to their parents' support. The commission suggested that these responsibilities were largely responsible for the failure of some Puerto Ricans to finish college.

Research indicates that working more than half-time, particularly at a campus job, has a positive effect.[14] This finding led to the recommendation "that if students are given financial aid in the form of work-study support, it be packaged in such a way that they work less than half time, and, whenever possible, at on-campus jobs.[15]

The national report also confirmed the findings of ASPIRA[16] that "the single most important factor contributions to the severe underrepresentation of Puerto Ricans (in the university) is their extremely high rate of attrition from secondary school. The second most important factor is the greater than average attrition from undergraduate colleges, particularly community colleges."[17] This is sad news, because it means that most Puerto Rican young people never really have a choice about attending college. If students have dropped out of high school, no amount of recruitment, however aggressive, can manufacture college potential. In other words, only about 40 percent of Puerto Rican young people will ever finish high school in the normal time span. A huge 60 percent of Puerto Ricans drop out, and will either be lost to higher education forever, or be forced to pass through several years of adult life before recognizing the need for education. That postponement of college is the present pattern, and as indicated above, is also responsible for the pressures of family and job becoming a major burden for a considerable number of our students. There can be little doubt that the effects of cutbacks in aid to the working poor under the Reagan Administration have affected a large percentage of Puerto Rican college students. Further trimming of veterans' benefits and aid to dependent children will also adversely affect those segments of Puerto Rican college enrollment that seek to return to studies and maintain a family while doing so.

The linkage between community college and four-year college is also likely to suffer. As indicated above, at the national level Puerto Ricans do not progress from community colleges to full baccalaureate colleges which may be explained by pressures from finances and family responsibility. However, the CUNY survey found a relatively high level of dissatisfaction with community colleges from the graduates in 1979. Some 34 percent desired a different CUNY college, contrasting with only 13 percent of four-year students who felt the same.[18] However, one in five of those with a Bachelor's degree from CUNY wished they had gone to a college outside CUNY. Additionally, roughly a third of all the minority graduates from CUNY wished they had gone to a college outside CUNY, and roughly a third of all the minority graduates from CUNY wished they had taken a different major. This probably reflects the depressed employment opportunities for education and social service majors—fields which have a major share of Puerto Rican students.[19]

Cumulatively, these data suggest that college counseling and recruitment agencies are not advising minorities correctly about college studies and the relationship to job opportunities.

The national survey suggested that higher quality of education increased the rate of minority success. In other words, the harder the college, the better the Puerto Rican student performs. Of course, both in CUNY as elsewhere, the community colleges are *de facto* recipients of the less capable high school graduates; prestigious Ivy League schools tend to recruit the best Puerto Rican students. But the deemphasis of affirmative action fostered by the Reagan administration, accompanied by cutbacks in aid to middle-class parents sending their children to private college may help public institutions such as CUNY. Since more Puerto Ricans may be forced for financial reasons to abandon plans to attend private colleges, these students may be more inclined to choose CUNY.

The question Puerto Rican studies must face, is how—if at all—our programs and departments can respond to the challenges presented by this profile to today's minority students. College administrators, especially those in CUNY, are concerned these days about falling enrollments. Any way in which Puerto Rican Studies add to students for the college is likely to receive a favorable hearing. More Puerto Rican students generally means more FTE's for Puerto Rican Studies and should safeguard the survival of departments and programs in a quantitative sense.

However, the larger issue concerns not quantity but quality. Puerto Rican Studies should not become a second home for students needing remedition or requiring counseling services the college can no longer afford to give them. To fall into this trap would be reinforce the role of inferior that the economic structure of US society assigns Puerto Ricans and other minorities. As Josephine Nieves pointed out, stratification of post-secondary institutions is becoming "more severe, and our students are tracked into dead-end careers." Since New York City now has a primarily finance, insurance, and real-estate economy,[20] the need for college-educated workers will probably increase. But will the Puerto Ricans who fill these jobs find themselves at the lowest rung of the pay-scale, just as their parents before them occupied the lower levels of the garment and manufacturing jobs, until these industries went into eclipse? The CUNY report shows no statistical difference in income separating minority Associate degree graduates from four-year graduates.[21] This seems to indicate that the majority of Puerto Ricans who graduate from CUNY with a Bachelor's degree cannot find significantly better jobs to recompense spending twice as many years in school as those with an Associate's degree. Moreover, in 1979, minority graduates were making less than $15,000 a year,[22] which would mean than if their spouse was not working, a Puerto Rican college graduate would earn less than the 1981 median U.S. family income. The CUNY report attributed these realities to minorities' preference for education and social service, which are low-paying fields.[23] It remains to be seen if Puerto Ricans who find jobs in the finance sector will differ notably from this low-salary pattern for present-day graduates. I believe that the current private-sector search for Hispanic business, marketing, and media executives provides an opportunity for Puerto Rican Studies.

The benefits of pursuing courses in our department and programs were always explained in terms of identification: for the Puerto Rican student to understand his or her Puerto Rican identity and to make some personal commitment of a professional career in service to the mass of Puerto Rican people who suffer from discrimination and various forms of oppression. The kind of knowledge offered by our department about the Puerto Rican people, therefore, carried with it a subjective dimension as well as objective information. The balancing of both the affective and cognitive aspects of knowledge is highly prized in the fields just mentioned. Major firms often look for persons with an intuitive grasp of the demographics of the Hispanic population and a "feel" for how the people think and react. This is and always has been a product of Puerto Rican Studies, as the conference participants pointed out in their different ways. It would be ironic if the defensive posture toward academia fostered by the cutbacks of the early 1980s enticed Puerto Rican Studies to abandon the very innovative approach to education that will be more highly prized in the future!

Our collective position as forerunners of an important new trend in education does not mean, however, that there is no need for adaptation. It would seem that most of our objective information about the Puerto Rican people has centered on past history and present sociological statistics, while the subjective identification has been rooted in humanistic studies and patriotic politics. It is probably necessary to weave into our courses scientific techniques for projecting the future of Puerto Ricans and other Hispanics. Should not demographics and the skill of interpreting economic projections be a part of Puerto Rican Studies? Ought not ecological concerns and the basics of energy engineering be included in our courses? These could be added to knowledge of migratory trends and studies in the Island's society and culture, so that the graduate's political commitments for the future of our people would be rounded out with reliable scientific projections.

Two obstacles to this development must be considered. One, our students are generally weak in the sciences because they lack a solid grounding in scientific thinking at the precollegiate level.[24] This is further complicated by the paucity of Puerto Rican educators presently on our faculties who have a science background. Moreover, studies on the scientific aspects of the Puerto Rican reality—reports on the ecological and energy necessities of the Island society and demographics of the state-side community—are infrequent. A major task, therefore, is to develop this information and an effective attachment to the Puerto Rican future that complements these projective sciences.

The other hitch to such a development takes on an ideological hue. Can Puerto Ricans be committed to social change if they work in today's corporate world? There can be little doubt that if the only reason to work at perfecting our students' grasp of projective science was to get them jobs in private industry, we would have been subverted by the dominant society that has oppressed our people. Education and social science lured our students in the past because these are careers that offered contact with the people and sometimes served as forums for preaching social change. This perception merits a challenge, however, because in addition to the decreasing number of opportunities in these sectors, one can seriously question whether the present educational or social service system are in fact forums for preaching social change. Despite the aspirations of most Puerto Rican educators and social workers, the apparatus of government often perpetuates discrimination. No one would suggest that this situation is totally hopeless. There are always ways to improve upon policy and institution.

It would seem, therefore, that if employment increases in the private sector, the same ingenuity that prepared students to turn government agencies to new purposes a decade ago should be brought to bear on the fields of finance management and communications today. Only a non-Marxist would pretend that social change does not depend upon control of the means of production. It must be explored if in tomorrow's New York, personnel management of white-collar workers may not offer more of a revolutionary potential than leadership in an evaporating garment-workers' union. Likewise, influence in the fabrication of the media image and appeal of Hispanics may exercise a powerful parallel force of education that should be turned to preserving Puerto Rican peoplehood.

This is a complex ideological issue that cannot be decided in these pages. But recent history suggests that an increasing number of Puerto Rican Studies' graduates are leaving the fields of social service and education for the corporate sector. They are forced into this decision by economic realities. Frequently, the switch in careers brings with it a "burn-out syndrome," in which the high aspirations for social change and a negative opinion of the business world engendered in Puerto Rican Studies combine to separate the Puerto Rican professional from past political commitments. Puerto Rican Studies will have to take these factors into account in whatever direction emerges as a collective strategy for encountering the contemporary reality of the Puerto Rican people.

Still another factor also requires attention. The national report aligns itself with the general goals of Puerto Rican Studies when it addresses the function of education.

> The principal function of all educational institutions should be to change people: to increase the competence of students, to enhance their personal development, and to help them lead more productive and fulfilling lives.[25]

This rationale suggests, therefore, that what Puerto Rican Studies has been doing within the departments and programs, is one of the functions of education. Unfortunately, administration's general passion for order generally leads the institutions to compartmentalize services, so that traditional departments only teach class materials and expect student services, counselors, and chaplains to contribute their pieces to an assembly-line university product. Thus, although we may well be doing the right thing as far as the students' development is concerned, our departments and programs tend to be perceived as the round peg in a square hole.

The national report suggest, however, that "educational institutions revise their testing and grading procedures to reflect and enhance the value-added mission."[26] Such a change in success criteria for education would, in effect, make the square holes round, forcing traditional departments to measure up to the functions of Puerto Rican Studies instead of vice versa. The commission highlights specific recommendations for such an alteration.

1) That current normative or relativistic measures be replaced by measures that assess the learning and growth of the individual student;
2) that these measures be administered periodically to assess the individuals growth over time;
3) that educational institutions enlarge their competency measures to include the assessment of growth in the non-cognitive realm: personal development, interpersonal skills, and self esteem.[27]

Such a task should not prove difficult for the majority of Puerto Rican Studies departments and programs, because such student development has always been a high priority. It might also be useful to anticipate the post-graduation problems, such as the burn-out syndrome, and cultivate successful Puerto Rican Studies alumni as role models and auxiliaries in the task of career selection.

In summary, if contextualization is the keynote to a rediscovery of a matrix for Puerto Rican Studies, then scientific orientation is the hallmark of applying our programs to the contemporary reality. This orientation applies principally to the need to link the natural, physical, social, and computer sciences to Puerto Rican Studies major graduates with the balance of cognitive and effective knowledge required for scientific projections that are highly prized by a widening sector of New York City's employers. At the same time, the personal development services generated by Puerto Rican Studies should be systematized and, whenever possible, be applied to the whole university enterprise. These developments should be accompanied by a thorough analysis of how corporate careers affect the collective struggle of Puerto Ricans to achieve their identity. Care must be taken not to identify a transition from a public service to private sector career with automatic "upward mobility," but neither should it be discounted as a focus for applying Puerto Rican Studies to the contemporary reality. Considering the contemporary reality, the renaissance of Puerto Rican Studies is already underway.

New Paradigms and Thought and Expression

The basic paradigm of Puerto Rican Studies is the interdisciplinary study of one people's reality. A well-designed area study that includes a mix of the sciences and the humanities is not fashionable in a widening circle of educational policy makers although the number of students expected to take part in these university studies is diminishing and specific attention to minority concerns is low priority.[28] What is required for a renaissance of Puerto Rican Studies, then, is not so much a recasting of the present thrust, but rather an integration of this solid paradigm into the agenda of university institutions. Illustration of this point is provided by the implementation at Brooklyn College of a core curriculum.

Restoration of basic required courses seems at first blush to be a return to the discredited goals of a past decade. In actuality, the implementation of the core curriculum at Brooklyn College proved to be an innovating experience. This result was achieved because the core curriculum required careful links in the progression of students from one course to another. The faculty involved in this project generally came to advocate the interdisciplinary approach as the paradigm of an authentic university education. The participation of Puerto Rican Studies in this project has been noteworthy, in that some of the department's suggestions were adopted. The net effect of the core curriculum at Brooklyn College has been to reduce the differences between Puerto Rican Studies and the general college without sacrificing our originality.

There are sound reasons to expect that concentration in a single area, such as that of Puerto Rican Studies, will find wider acceptance. Traditionally, students were expected to take a series of general courses in a particular field and after mastering this universal knowledge, were then allowed to choose a single area in which to specialize. Actually, the human mind learns in a process that is exactly the reverse. The mind conceptualizes the universal by comparing specific cases and constructing applicable abstractions.

Thus, area studies logically precede a general knowledge of sociology, history, and the like. Were we able to make utopian expectations of the university, students would take area studies first and spend their last semester in theoretic courses intended to provide a general explanation. In any case, adoption of area studies is a viable path to relevant abstractions about society and its people, and provides an undeniable advantage to Puerto Rican Studies in the struggle for academic respectability.

The student ought to be able to see in the particularity of Puerto Rican Studies some means of comparison to other experiences. For instance, does a history class in Puerto Rican Studies help the students to grasp the nature of the movement in our literature? Does the student understand how the Puerto Rican experience compares with a similar process in places as varied as Cuba, France, or Ireland? The contextualization and the interdisciplinary approaches are complementary: with contextualization, we enrich to content of our courses; in the interdisciplinary approach, our class materials are cast in categories that are applicable to a wide range of experiences. The interdisciplinary approach critically integrates different disciplines in understanding the complexity of human experience. The burden for this association should not fall exclusively to the student, but should be designed by faculty as a part of the learning process. The study of history in the Puerto Rican Studies Department has to be concerned with the students' ability to grasp literature, even if the historian does not teach literature in his or her class load. Likewise, the sociologist in the department must recognize, for instance, that music has a role in contemporary Puerto Rican social identity that must fit into the students' grasp of social forces at work in the Puerto Rican experience.

Observations such as these show the validity of Frank Bonilla's comments in 1973. He foresaw a move from a simple affirmation of Puerto Rican reality that was "largely of a defensive nature" toward one with "a much more extensive profound and disciplined drive toward self-definition and power in motion."[29]

Professor Patrick Hill's remarks highlight the opportunity offered Puerto Rican Studies to utilize its basic interdisciplinary and area study nature as wellsprings for authenticity. He suggests that general education has moved in these directions because of the sterility of traditional undergraduate studies. Hence, in principle, the "new paradigm of thought and experience" provided by Puerto Rican Studies augurs for a renaissance, not only of our departments and programs, but the whole university as well. One hastens to add, however, that because our goals are intertwined with a general university reform opposition to innovation will increase. The insights of Frank Bonilla a decade ago, bear repeating.

That sense of threat is without doubt compounded by the fact that the Puerto Rican drive for a place in the university occurs in the context of a larger institutional crisis and a reaction to that crisis. The university is a centuries-old social invention with various functions, including a primary commitment to some freedom in the creation and sharing of knowledge. In practice it has been much concerned with establishing proprietary rights over knowledge. . . . The mood at the top in major institutions is one of retrenchment; the formula is to tighten security measures and hold the line, or, where possible, to turn the clock back.[30]

What is in conflict are two different world views—*epistemologies,* as Bonilla calls them. This remains the same in 1982 as it was in 1973—but the new factor is the inability of CUNY to function without Puerto Rican students. Hence, whereas a decade ago reactionary forces in academia fought to expel our students by impossible demands upon their skills or to "marginate" them into majors or careers that were perceived as provincial or unattractive, the battle ground has shifted today. Now even conservatives hope to keep our students on campus and attempt to bring them into their own disciplines. Hence, the emergence on campus of a "conservative" Puerto Rican, or students with little or no awareness of the value of a national consciousness, must not be underestimated.

Puerto Rican Studies, I submit, has a valuable and relevant paradigm for thought and expression, but one whose future is now dependent on the conflict for ideological control of higher education now taking place in the university of the country. For better or worse, Puerto Rican Students will be a part of CUNY, but the bonds between these students and Puerto Rican studies are not automatic. A renaissance of Puerto Rican Studies will be possible wherever our interdisciplinary approach is found in coalition with other progressive forces in the university and where, simultaneously, our program and departments offer a curriculum that puts the Puerto Rican experience in context with the global community.

The new directions for Puerto Rican Studies must include outreach to the community. The disastrous high school dropout rates for Puerto Ricans make it essential that recruitment of students for colleges, especially for CUNY, ought to figure highly in the priorities for community action by Puerto Rican Studies. As already stated, the need for FTE's in CUNY makes it possible for Puerto Rican faculty to enter easily into recruitment efforts. What is not so easy to achieve is a specifically Puerto Rican appeal, so that the entering freshman have expectations of becoming more complete Puerto Rican, rather than merely successful graduates. Unless students see our program and departments as stepping-stones of achievement of their goals, we are not likely to profit directly from increased Puerto Rican student enrollment.

A great resource in the effort to project a positive image for Puerto Rican Studies for prospective freshmen is our alumni. With nearly a decade of history, some of our graduates are now holding important positions in schools, agencies, and businesses. Despite its drawbacks as an institution, CUNY has served the present generation of Puerto Ricans in New York as the prelude to successful visibility in the city, much as the university also provided other groups with a similar opportunity a generation ago. These alumni ought to be recruited wherever possible as participants in the struggle for visibility.

The community ties with the university are also being given a more important role because of the budget cuts initiated in the early 1980s by the Reagan Administration. The university setting may become a key platform for expounding the particularized needs of the Puerto Rican people. As funding dries up for such stalwart agencies, such as ASPIRA and the Puerto Rican Forum, their functions are reduced. Experimentation with policy innovations and opportunities for research projects outside the university setting are thus in jeopardy, and the 1980s will probably see a greater reliance by the community upon Puerto Rican scholars for information about the Puerto Rican experience.

Unfortunately, we are relatively unprepared as a university faculty for this challenge. There is no scholarly journal for Puerto Rican Studies that can provide serious comment on our social situation. There is no association of Puerto Rican university educators who could sponsor such a publication, or even provide a forum for professional exchange at an annual conference. Except for individual initiative, there is no clear connection between Puerto Rican scholars and the several political officials of federal, state, and local governments. Without some or all of these outlets for collective creativity, it is unlikely that a renaissance will come to Puerto Rican Studies except in fits and spurts.

Puerto Rican Studies desperately needs to discover the instruments for ongoing dialog with its component parts and to compare notes with similar academic efforts, especially Chicano Studies. UCLA's Center for Chicano Studies' publication, *Atzlan*, as well as the companion association for Chicano educators represents a rich resource without immediate parallel within Puerto Rican Studies. Nonetheless, there is sufficient vitality within our programs and departments to suggest that the development of such resources is feasible. Moreover, when a publication and association appear, they will greatly strengthen the bonds between Puerto Rican Studies and the community because they will provide a touchpoint of contact with a wide spectrum of grass-roots and government leadership.

Josephine Nieves alluded to the frictions caused when the political agenda of Puerto Rico was imported to New York without sufficient forethought. The needs and aspirations of Puerto Ricans in the continental United States were not always clearly reflected in the projections provided by the Island-oriented faculty. Moreover, in some cases there was a hint of islander's arrogance toward the city-raised Puerto Rican, both student and faculty. Often the attitudes engendered by these conflicts were based on class differences.

In the 1980s, however, most Puerto Rican Studies entities in the States have achieved a working solution to these islander-statesider conflicts. What must be achieved for a renaissance is a more aggressive exchange between progressive elements in Puerto Rico and Puerto Rican Studies here. For instance, the typical Puerto Rican islander who graduates knows very little from university education about the Puerto Rican migration, the sociological situation of 40 percent of the Puerto Rican people, or the cultural persistance of Puerto Rican Studies on the continent. This ignorance complicates the islander attitude toward the Puerto Ricans who have gone north.

The major universities of Puerto Rico probably need a course of studies on the non-Island Puerto Rican community, so that knowledge of the stateside reality will play a more significant part in Puerto Rican society. Why are there not courses at the University of Puerto Rico in the history, sociology, political development, art, music, and literature of the Puerto Ricans of New York, much as at CUNY there are such courses on the Island experience? It is unlikely during the collapse of the Puerto Rican economy that the Island's institutions of higher learning will generate any initiative on these lines. However, Puerto Rican Studies should and probably could make a contribution to the Island's higher education system by a careful and well thought out effort. However, there is need to "strategize" about such institutional links as well as for input into the various scholarly and professionals academic associations of Puerto Rico. Nonetheless, the renaissance of Puerto Rican Studies implies that our paradigm of thought and expression has matured enough to be introduced into Puerto Rico.

Summary

The question returns, "Is there a renaissance of Puerto Rican Studies?" There definitely seems to be a movement toward the contextualization of our curriculum into a richer setting of comparative studies. But this contextualization has still not matured sufficiently for us to feel that we have articulated the matrix of Puerto Rican

Studies that would guarantee the flowering of a renaissance. Nonetheless, we are closer to this moment than we were when we started with much aggressiveness to insist upon our particularity as a people and an oppressed nation. If we avoid the pitfalls of a shallow cultural pluralism, Puerto Rican Studies should be able to gain respectability for itself within the university.

The contemporary reality of higher education for minorities and for CUNY have afforded Puerto Rican Studies a magnificent opportunity to apply the lessons of a decade to the present day. This essay has suggested that a scientific measurement of the humanistic value of our educational programs would strengthen the affective dimension of higher education. At the same time, a shift to careers in the private sector requires a retooling of our curriculum so that projective sciences can enrich our students' ideological analysis, as well as provide the scientific tools utilized for such courses of study.

Our interdisciplinary paradigm is in great demand, although the need for constant development persists. Maintenance of our educational approach aligns us with the progressive forces within higher education today. However, such a posture also presents dangers that Puerto Rican Studies will be perceived by even Puerto Rican students as a needlessly politicized program detached from basic college education.

The ties between Puerto Rican Studies and the Puerto Rican community require a greater breadth and a closer coordination with policy needs and responsible leaders. Such a development will be impeded by the absence of a quality journal or professional association to provide a point of contact with our community's leadership. Moreover, we have a worthwhile message to share with the Island's educational apparatus.

Hence, the renaissance of Puerto Rican Studies is already present in a series of challenges, opportunities, and general trends. What is lacking is a sense of direction and a heady confidence on the part of Puerto Rican Studies that our collective energies are indeed a part of a general progressive force.

This intangible feeling can marshall the ambivalent forces swimming about us into a wave of renaissance. Strong leadership summoning forth collective efforts will produce the means of serious scholarly exchange. This is the required ingredient to transform Puerto Rican Studies that will bring about a true renaissance.

Notes

1. Joshua A. Fishman, *Bilingual Education: An International Sociological Perspective*, p. 17.

Ethnic Distributions of Bachelor Enrollees and Graduates: A Comparison of CUNY and National Data

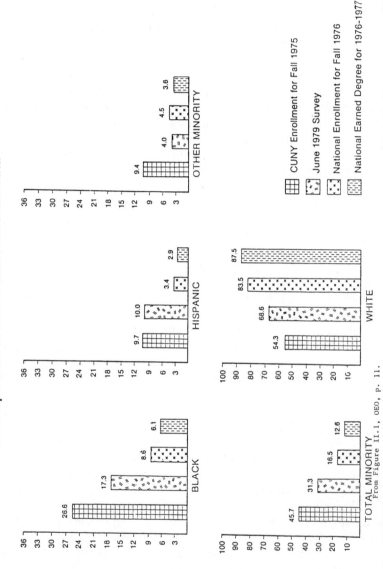

From Figure II.1, OEO, p. 11.

Legend:
- ⊞ CUNY Enrollment for Fall 1975
- ▨ June 1979 Survey
- ▦ National Enrollment for Fall 1976
- ▥ National Earned Degree for 1976-1977

2. Marie Ferrer Iturriano, ed., *A New Look at the Puerto Rican Studies and their Society*, p. 74.

3. Centro, Labor Manager, pp. 16–26.

4. Ferrer Iturriano, p. 74.

5. Alexander W. Austin, *Final Report of the Commission: The Higher Educator of Minorities*.

6. Barry Kaufman, James Murtha, and Jerzy Warman, *Outcomes of Educational Opportunity: a Study of Graduates from the City University*, CUNY; Clara Rodriguez, "Triple Jeopardy and an Ethnic Studies Department," Arturo Cabrera, *The Minority Administrator in Higher Education*, pp. 71–80.

7. OEO, Figure II.2.

8. *Ibid.*, Table III, 6, p. 38.

DISTRIBUTION OF GRADE POINT AVERAGES (GPA) BY DEGREE

GPA	Associates	Bachelors	Total
Less than 2.50	33.0	19.9	24.8
2.50 - 2.99	31.3	30.3	30.7
3.00 - 3.49	26.1	31.6	29.5
3.50 - 4.00	9.6	18.2	15.0
Total %	100.0	100.0	100.0
(N)	(554)	(913)	(1467)

9. *Ibid.*, Table III, 5, p. 37.

NUMBER OF REMEDIAL COURSE HOURS BY DEGREE

Remedial Hours	Associates	Bachelors	Total
None	32.1	48.7	42.5
1 - 6 hours	32.8	40.4	37.5
7 - 12 hours	17.7	6.7	10.9
13 or more hours	17.4	4.2	9.2
Total %	100.0	100.0	100.0
(N)	(554)	(913)	(1467)

10. *Ibid.*, p. 14.

11. *Ibid.*, p. 15.

12. *Ibid.*, pp. 16–17.

13. HEM, p. 31.

14. A. J. Austin and P. H. Cross, *Student Financial Aid and Persistence in College.*

15. HEM, p. 3.

16. *Ibid.*

17. *Ibid.*, p. 17.

18. OEO, Table V.4, p. 64.

SATISFACTION WITH UNDERGRADUATE COLLEGE AND PROGRAM CHOICE
BY DEGREE

Item	Associates	Bachelors
Would you enroll in college again?		
Yes	98.9	96.6
No	1.1	3.4
Total %	100.0	100.0
(N)	(301)	(500)
Would you enroll in the same major/program?		
Same	62.3	68.3
Different	37.7	31.7
Total %	100.0	100.0
(N)	(295)	(476)
Would you enroll in the same college?		
Yes	56.1	65.3
No, different CUNY college	34.1	13.1
No, a college outside CUNY	9.8	21.7
Total %	100.0	100.0
(N)	(296)	(470)

19. HEM, p. 17.

20. Bureau of Labor Statistics, *Mid-year Review*, July 1982.

21. OEO, p. 47.

22. *Ibid.*, p. 45.

23. *Ibid.*, p. 46.

24. HEM, p. 18.

25. *Ibid.*, p. 25.

26. *Ibid.*, p. 24.

27. *Ibid.*, pp. 24–25.

28. R. Glover and B. Gross, *Report on the National Forum on Learning in the Future Needs and Goals for Adult Learning, 1980–2000.*

29. Bonilla, p. 227.

30. *Ibid.*, pp. 230–31.

APPENDIX

Puerto Rican Studies Curriculum of Brooklyn College

General Description

The Department offers a comprehensive program leading to a major in Puerto Rican Studies and a baccalaureate degree. Course offerings reflect the Puerto Rican reality on the island and the United States via a multi-disciplinary approach. These are grouped in the following areas: culture and the arts, history and literature, bilingualism and education, contemporary society, and specialized seminars. Demonstrated knowledge of Spanish by the end of the junior year is required of majors.

The Puerto Rican Studies Department offers courses for elementary education majors interested in teaching Spanish-speaking children. Students may qualify for certification in bilingual education by completing the sequence of courses approved and advised by the counselors in the School of Education, the Puerto Rican Studies Department, and other appropriate departments.

The Department is co-sponsor of the Caribbean Studies Program, an interdisciplinary dual major offered jointly with the African Studies Department and in collaboration with other departments in the area of social sciences. The Department also participates in the college's core curriculum via Core Studies 9, Studies in African, Asian, and Latin American Cultures.

The Department offers courses in the graduate history division. A Puerto Rican Studies graduate course sequence in education is required for students in the Master's program leading to a degree in elementary education with a bilingual specialization. Puerto Rican Studies graduate courses in literature may be taken to fulfill requirements in the Master of Arts degree program in Spanish offered in the Modern Languages and Literature Department.

Courses Dealing with the Puerto Rican Experience

Introduction to Puerto Rican Studies

Survey of Puerto Rican studies. Pertinent themes in Puerto Rican history, culture, literature, contemporary society, and politics. Impact of United States' economic policies on the Island and causes of Puerto Rican migration to urban centers on the continent. Puerto Ricans in New York City.

Puerto Rican Cultural Patterns I

Cultural antecedents and development of present Puerto Rican culture. Pre-Columbian contributions, European and African elements, Puerto Rican folklore and cultural patterns, perspectives on Puerto Rican national culture.

Taino Roots of Contemporary Religion and Culture in Puerto Rico and the Caribbean

Religious artifacts and cultural system of pre-Columbian inhabitants of Puerto Rico and other Caribbean islands, from neolithic times to European colonization. Taino myths and the principal elements of religion. Indigenous influences in contemporary societies and as a theme of national identity.

Puerto Rican Cultural Patterns II

Disruptive effects of migration to New York in relation to the values, mores, and beliefs of the Puerto Rican people. Cultural issues related to colonialism, race, and identity. Evaluation of research methodology used in the studies of Puerto Rican cultural patterns.

Spiritism and African Religions in Puerto Rican Culture

African heritage as a religious and cultural phenomenon in Puerto Rico. Contemporary Afro-Caribbean folk religions and cults, *"Espiritismo,"* *"Santeria,"* and their effects on Puerto Ricans today.

Artistic Expression and Symbolism of the Puerto Rican People

Development of artistic expression and symbolism among Puerto Ricans from Taino society until the present. Puerto Rican identity and folklore.

Music of the Puerto Rican People

Survey of folk, popular, classical forms of Puerto Rican music. Influence of Taino Indian, Spanish, and Black cultures on these forms. Relationship between Puerto Rican music and folklore. Lectures supplemented with performances, slides, tapes, records.

Women in Puerto Rican Society

Roles of women in different historical periods. Biographies and documents. Literary works by women who broke with traditions and social constraints. Current research, government, politics, and the labor force.

History of Puerto Rico to 1815

Pre-Columbian to 1815. Indians of Puerto Rico and their encounters with Western culture. First centuries under Spanish rule. Contributions of Spain and Spanish heritage to Puerto Rican history. Slavery. Early historical figures. Impact of the Enlightenment and Latin American independence upon Puerto Rican history.

History of Puerto Rico since 1815

Cedula de Gracia. Lares Rebellion of 1868. Puerto Rican political parties. Spanish repression. Emergence of a Puerto Rican national consciousness reflected in political and social institutions. Leaders such as Muñoz Rivera, Barbosa, de Diego, and Albizu Campos. United States occupation and modification of colonial institutions. Operation Bootstrap and industrialization of the Island under Commonwealth status.

The Puerto Rican Community in the United States: Settlement and Evolution

Puerto Rican migrants to the United States and the development of representative institutions. Historical role of agencies and leaders. Puerto Rican settlement patterns throughout the United States compared with New York. Historical similarities and differences of Puerto Ricans and other groups.

Survey of Puerto Rican Literature

Reading and discussion of significant literature by Puerto Rican authors writing in Spanish and English.

Puerto Rican Poetry from the Aguinaldo to the Present

Poetry of Puerto Ricans on the Island and in the United States. Language as a major preoccupation in the struggle against cultural penetration. Works by such authors as Gautier Benitez, Lloréns Torres, Rivera Chevremont, Palés Matos, Matos Paoli, Corretjer, de Burgos, Margenat, Soto Vélez, and the poets of the contemporary urban experience.

Survey of Puerto Rican Drama and Theater

Puerto Rican culture in its theater and drama. Historical development of drama and contemporary theater. Special emphasis upon New York City's art and theater groups.

Puerto Rican Narrative

Puerto Rican narrative from the nineteenth century and its development as a major expression for social protest on the Island and in New York. Detailed study of novels and short stories by Alonso, Zeno Gandía, Marqués, Díaz Alfaro, Laguerre, José Luis González, Pedro Juan Soto, Rosario Ferré, and others.

Black Expression in Caribbean Literature

Black culture and writings in the Caribbean. Reflections on alienation and independence. Literary liberation movements, Negrism, Indigenism, and *Negritude* as first emancipations from a European cultural vision. Writers from the English-, French-, and Spanish-speaking countries will be examined.

The Puerto Rican, Hispanic, and Caribbean Child in the New York City Educational System

Puerto Ricans, Hispanics, and Caribbeans in contemporary society. Relation of school curricula to their historical background and cultural contributions. Development of identity, knowledge, and appreciation of heritage. Examination, use, and evaluation of instructional materials. Concepts, information, and material necessary for effective work and quality education for the target population in the school system. Field work.

Bilingualism: The Puerto Rican, Caribbean, and Hispanic American Child

Concepts and programs of bilingualism. Their importance and application to the education of multi-ethnic school populations. Selected field and laboratory work; study and evaluation of bilingual programs and materials.

Spanish Language Arts for the Bilingual Child

Fundamental concepts of Puerto Rican and other regional patterns of the Spanish language and literature for the prospective teacher. Spanish language arts applied to the bilingual child.

English as a Second Language

Role of English as a second language for the Puerto Rican and other Spanish-speaking children in a bilingual program. Comparative analysis, understanding linguistic concepts, and their application. Field experience related to language patterns of bilingual children.

Puerto Rican and Hispanic History and Culture for the Teacher

History and culture of Puerto Rican and other Hispanic groups for prospective teachers. Preparation of materials for Puerto Rican and other Hispanic groups, assessment, models. Field experience in educational and cultural institutions.

Introduction to Spanish for Prospective Bilingual Teachers

Structure of the Spanish language. Practice in Puerto Rican and other regional idiomatic expressions. This course is intended for prospective bilingual teachers.

Economic Development of Puerto Rico and Migration under Capitalism

Colonial basis for the development of capitalism in Puerto Rico in the twentieth century. Key factors stimulating growth and dependency after 1948. Diffusion of Puerto Ricans in New York City and other urban centers. Integration of the economies of Puerto Rico and the United States and implications for future policy making.

Government and Politics of Puerto Rico

Puerto Rican political system. Constitutional structure and administrative systems. Contemporary political status and present political party structures.

Impact of Social Service Systems on the
Puerto Rican, Black, and Other Urban Populations

Development of social welfare legislation from the poor laws to the present. Implications for the poor in New York and other urban centers. Concept of client participation and control of social services. Government programs and institutions affecting Puerto Ricans on the mainland, Black, Caribbean, and Hispanic migrants to the city.

Administration of Justice and the Puerto Rican Community

Relationship of Puerto Ricans in the United States to the police and the courts. The prison system and legal assistance. Juvenile delinquency, drugs, and crime. Class action suits, community progress and litigation, organized movements.

Behavioral Patterns of Puerto Ricans
in the United States

Cultural concepts pertinent to understanding the Puerto Rican community in the United States. Mental health care, counseling needs, and family systems.

Community Organization and Service to
the Puerto Rican Community

Basic community organization theory and development of practical skills for service to Puerto Rican and other Hispanic communities. Readings, lectures, and examination of case records. Motivation for self-help programs. Contact with internal operations of Puerto Rican organizations and appraisal of their varied approaches and techniques. Supervised field work with organizations that serve the Puerto Rican community.

The Aged Among Puerto Ricans and Other Hispanics

Present conditions of Hispanic aged. Theoretical concerns. Social intervention and services. Hispanic aged and their share of social and economic resources within the American mainstream.

Seminar in Political, Social, and
Economic Status of Puerto Rico

Political, social, and economic structures in Puerto Rico. Analysis of congressional policies. U.N. decolonization process and Puerto Rico. Effects of political status in social and economic terms.

Special Topics

Topics vary from term to term. Course description may be obtained in the department office before registration. Topics may include social problems, social institutions, social processes, social organizations of Puerto Ricans in Puerto Rico and the United States.

Seminar in the Nationalist Movements of Puerto Rico

Historical antecedents of the present nationalism movements in Puerto Rico. Evolution of colonial society into a national entity, conspiracies of the early nineteenth century, *El Grito de Lares* and Betances' leadership and solidarity with Cuban revolutionary movements. Independence, parties in electoral politics, the Nationalist Party and Albizu Campos' political philosophy. Impact of McCarthyism and the Cuban revolution on Puerto Rican politics. Present ideologies, parties, and social classes in the independence movement.

Summer Seminar in Puerto Rico

In cooperation with a University or other institution of higher education in Puerto Rico, the United States, the Hispanic Caribbean or Latin America, the department offers opportunities for advanced work in Puerto Rican studies. Supervised field trips to places of cultural and historical significance. Lectures by scholars from Brooklyn College and host country. Independent and/or group research.

Emerging Realities and Alternatives for Puerto Ricans and other Hispanics in the United States

Demographic and political trends of Hispanics in the United States and the impact on Puerto Ricans. Education, labor organizations, public services, economic development, political power, and future challenges to Hispanics. Alternatives for Puerto Ricans in a Caribbean context and the impact of a change in political status of the Island upon Puerto Ricans in the United States.

Independent Study I, II

Independent study supervised by a Faculty member. Approved topic. Periodic conferences. Report.

Graduate Program

Puerto Rico: History of Political Dependence
from 1493 to 1917

Puerto Rico as a national unit within Latin America and a case study in colonialism. The making of a Spanish colony. Political movements in Puerto Rico and elsewhere in Latin America in the eighteenth and nineteenth centuries. Spain and the United States in the Caribbean: comparison of their colonial rule. Ties between political movements in the United States and Puerto Rico.

Puerto Rico: History of Political Dependence
from 1917 to the Present

Political movements from 1917 to 1932: *La Coalición*, Liberals, Republicans, Socialists, and the rise of the Nationalists. The Populares and the Commonwealth: Operation Bootstrap, emigration, the 1967 plesbicite. New independence movements, Puerto Rico, Latin America, the Cuban Revolution, and the Third World Movement.

Puerto Rican Society

Puerto Rican society. Colonial conditions necessary for understanding Puerto Rican society. Social reality in Puerto Rico in terms of foreign and native images. Social interpretation of historical processes with regard to trends and attributes accepted, transmitted, and developed in society.

Social Institutions in Puerto Rico

Principal social institutions. The family, economic, educational, political systems; the system of belief and religious practice. Sociohistorical approach to inquiries into origins, development, present functioning of selected institutions. Reciprocal interrelationship of the institutional setting. Impact of the new social process on various institutions. Impact of each institution on Puerto Ricans, particularly with regard to determining normality and abnormality in Puerto Rico.

Bilingualism: Characteristics and Practices

Philosophy and general practices related to bilingual programs in the United States. New theories, writings, research studies in linguistic and psycholinguistics. Application centered on the psychosociological background for language development in Puerto Rican children. Bilingual schools and programs.

Puerto Rican Communities in Urban Areas

History of the social, political, cultural development of Puerto Ricans in the United States. Population distribution in urban areas. The New York community. Detailed analysis and evaluation of institutions attempting to serve Puerto Ricans.

Puerto Rican Narrative and Drama

Detailed study of the structure and content of Puerto Rican short stories, novels, plays, in relation to the colonial history of the Island and its sociological and psychological impact on the Puerto Rican. Such writers of the nineteenth and twentieth centuries as Betances, Tapia, Zeno Gandía, Laguerre, Méndez Ballester, Andreu, Arriví, Marqués, González, Soto, Varcarcel, Sanchez. This course is conducted in Spanish.

Puerto Rican Poetry and Essay

Important currents of thought in the Puerto Rican essay and poetry and their relation to the struggle for the liberation of Puerto Rico. Romanticism and Modernism. New indigenous schools. Writers include Alonso, Gautier, Betances, de Hostos, de Diego, Lloráens, Pedreira, Palés, Albizu, Corretjer, Matos Paoli, Maldonado, Silén, the generation of Guajana and Mester, Pietri, Hernández, Rosario. This course is conducted in Spanish.

Center for Latino Studies

The Center is an adjunct of the Department of Puerto Rican Studies. It serves students, faculty, and the community by stimulating interest in Puerto Rican and Latino affairs. It provides opportunities to sponsor conferences, workshops, lectures, seminars, internships, and noncredit courses. It encourages curricular development on topics related to the Latino experience; fosters educational exhibits, as well as artistic and cultural expression. The center maintains a facility for career and academic information, special collections, publications and research.

Glossary

Atzlan. Name of the region in the present-day United States from which the Aztecs were supposed to have migrated toward Mexico. The term is used among Chicanos as a poetic symbol of cultural and political sovereignty.

ASPIRA. An educational agency founded in New York City in 1961 by Puerto Ricans to facilitate the entry of Puerto Rican students into college. Its programs provided classes which heightened the cultural awareness of the Puerto Rican heritage and a pride in ethnic identity.

Blades, Rubén. A Panamanian composer-singer of contemporary popular music that praises Puerto Rican and Latin American cultural identity.

Boricua. Alternate name for a Puerto Rican, derived from the pre-Columbian language.

Centro de Estudios Puertorriqueños [Center for Puerto Rican Studies]. A research center, affiliated with the City University of New York, which develops curriculum and conducts research on the Puerto Ricans in the United States.

CEREP—*Centro de Estudios de la Realidad Puertorriqueña* [Center for the Study of the Puerto Rican Reality]. An Island-based association of social scientists dedicated to exploring the nature of Puerto Rican society from creative perspectives.

Chicano. A term used to designate people of Mexican descent born in the United States, and who have acquired a social and political conscience.

Commonwealth. The present political relation between Puerto Rico and the United States. It provides autonomy in local internal matters for the Puerto Rican elected officials, while retaining constitutional and federal control for Washington. Puerto Ricans are citizens of the

United States, but those resident on the Island do not vote in national elections.

Colon, Jesus (1901–1971). A black Puerto Rican labor organizer, who wrote for *The Daily Worker*, and whose short stories of life in New York during the Depression are considered early examples of literary expression by Puerto Ricans in English.

Freire, Paolo. A contemporary Brazilian educator who developed a method of mass adult education by fostering a social and political consciousness among the poor.

FTE—Faculty Teaching Equivalent. A standard measure of the ratio between the number of students taught in each hour of an instructor's classroom lecture.

FUPI—*Federación Universitaria Pro-Independencia*. A student organization for Puerto Ricans who advocate independence for the Island from the United States.

Hispanic. A generic term for all peoples of Ibero-American heritage resident in the United States.

Kibee, Robert. Chancellor of the City University of New York (CUNY), from October 1, 1971 until his death on June 16, 1982.

Mayagüez. A large city on Puerto Rico's western coast, site of the public university for engineering, generally considered the finest unit of the Island's higher education system.

NABE—National Association of Bilingual Educators.

Native Americans. A term used to describe the pre-Columbian inhabitants of the Western Hemisphere. This name is considered more precise than "Indians."

Neorican. A term to describe persons of Puerto Rican ancestry born in the United States.

NIMH—National Institute on Mental Health. A federal agency that has funded various studies related to culturally motivated behavior.

Pedreira, Antonio S. (1905–1959). Puerto Rican educator and commentator on themes of Puerto Rican culture.

PRACA—Puerto Rican Association for Community Action. A New York City-based agency run by Puerto Ricans that coordinates social service delivery.

PRCDP—Puerto Rican Community Development Project. A city agency founded in 1965 to supervise the dispensing of social services to Puerto Ricans.

PREA—Puerto Rican Educators Association. An organization for Puerto Rican teachers and other educators in the New York city Area.

Puerto Rican Migration Research Consortium. An association of Puerto Rican social scientists interested in coordinating research on Puerto Ricans who have migrated to the United States.

SABE—State Association of Bilingual Educators.

Schomberg Collection. An extensive archives, housed in the Harlem section of New York, initiated by the black Puerto Rican musicologist, Arturo Schomberg (1874–1938).

The Rican. The name of a magazine published in Chicago which focused on the emerging social and cultural reality of Puerto Ricans born in the United States.

Young Lords' Party. A militant youth organization of Hispanics, which was successful in using confrontational tactics to secure opportunities for Puerto Ricans from official agencies and institutions during the late 1960s and early 1970s.

Vega, Bernardo (1886–1965). A Puerto Rican cigar maker, who migrated to New York City in 1916 and was active in the formation of various Puerto Rican labor and community associations when the number of Puerto Rican migrants in New York City was limited.

Vieques. An island municipality of Puerto Rico where the United States Navy maintains a proving grounds. The town has been the scene of confrontations between local residents and the Navy during maneuvers in which the island was used for target practice.

West Side Story. A 1950s Broadway musical, loosely patterned on the love story of Romeo and Juliet, that used the racial and ethnic tensions in Manhattan between Puerto Rican and other ethnic groups as a backdrop for a love story that ends in tragedy.

List of Contributors

Eduardo Aponte. Professor, the University of Puerto Rico; Assistant Director, Council of Higher Education; former member of the Department of Puerto Rican Studies, Brooklyn College.

Frank Bonilla. Head of the *Centro de Estudios Puertorriqueños* at Hunter College, the City University of New York research center for Puerto Rican Studies; Prof. Bonilla has been an important guide in the self-examination of Puerto Rican Studies.

Pedro Cabán. Assistant Professor of Political Science at Fordham University, Rose Hill Campus.

Loida Figueroa Mercado. Professor, the University of Puerto Rico at Mayaguez, formerly member of the faculty of Puerto Rican Studies at Brooklyn College, Prof. Figueroa Mercado is the author of several books on the history of Puerto Rico, including one widely used as a text in Puerto Rican Studies programs.

José Hernández. Professor and Coordinator of Puerto Rican Studies at Hunter College. Formerly Research Director at the Latino Institute in Chicago and Professor of Sociology at the University of Wisconsin. Author of *Puerto Rican Youth Employment* and the ASPIRA report on *Social Factors in the Educational Attainment of Puerto Ricans*; directed the U.S. Civil Rights Commission project on *Social Indicators of Equality for Minorities and Women*.

Juan E. Hernández Cruz. Formerly Professor of Puerto Rican Studies at Brooklyn College and former Director of the Puerto Rican Studies Program at Fordham University, Prof. Hernández Cruz is presently Dean of the Interamerican University in San German, Puerto Rico.

Janice Gordils. Formerly Professor in the Department of Modern Languages, Fordham University at Lincoln Center; Prof. Gordils is presently on the faculty of the University of Puerto Rico, Cayey campus.

Patrick J. Hill. Formerly Director of the Federated Learning Community at the State University of New York, Stoney Brook, Director Hill is now Provost at Evergreen College.

James Jennings. Associate Professor, The University of Massachusetts-Boston; Co-editor *Puerto-Rican Politics in Urban America* (Greenwood Press, 1984) and *From Access to Power: Black Politics in Boston* (Schenkmar Books, 1986).

Julio Morales. Former member of the Department of Puerto Rican Studies, Brooklyn College, Prof. Morales is presently at the Graduate School of Social Work of the University of Connecticut, where he has developed a series of courses designed to prepare Puerto Ricans to understand social work and community service.

Sonia Nieto. Former member of the faculty of Puerto Rican Studies, Brooklyn College, Prof. Nieto is presently at the University of Massachusetts-Amherst.

Josephine Nieves. The first chairperson of the Department of Puerto Rican Studies at Brooklyn College, Prof. Nieves is a leading force in community organization and a respected public administrator, having served as head of the Community Services Administration. At present she is Assistant General Director at the Community Services Society in New York. Her paper in this volume is a condensation of an address originally written by Maria Canino, Sherry Gorelick, Josephine Nieves, Hildamar Ortiz, Camile Rodriquez, and Jesse Vázquez.

Rafael L. Ramírez. Professor of Anthropology, the University of Puerto Rico, Rio Piedras.

Maria E. Sanchez. Chairperson of the Department of Puerto Rican Studies, Brooklyn College, Prof. Sanchez has an extensive background in teaching, educational administration, and supervision at various levels in the New York City educational system, including service as Supervisor of Bilingual Programs.

Antonio M. Stevens-Arroyo. Associate Professor of Puerto Rican Studies, Brooklyn College, Prof. Stevens-Arroyo is the author of an award-winning study of the Hispanic church, *Prophets Denied Honor* (Orbis: 1980). He has served as Deputy Chairman of the Advisory Committee to the United States Commission on Civil Rights and has published extensively on a variety of themes on culture and civilization.

Andrés Torres. Former student activist; presently graduate student in Economics at the New School for Social Research, and Director

of the History and Migration Task Force, Centro de Estudios Puertorriqueños.

Jesse M. Vázquez. Director, the Puerto Rican Studies Program, Queens
College, and Assistant Professor, Department of Graduate Educational
and Community Programs in the School of Education.